BIOGRAPHY OF AN Organizer

A TRUE STORY

YOANN PESANT

BIOGRAPHY OF AN ORGANIZER
A TRUE STORY

iUniverse books may be ordered through booksellers or by contacting:

iUniverse
1663 Liberty Drive
Bloomington, IN 47403
www.iuniverse.com
1-800-Authors (1-800-288-4677)

ISBN: 978-1-5320-8897-1 (sc)
ISBN: 978-1-5320-8899-5 (hc)
ISBN: 978-1-5320-8898-8 (e)

Library of Congress Control Number: 2019920643

Print information available on the last page.

iUniverse rev. date: 12/23/2019

Acknowledgments

Creed of Thanks

To all the Club Vacation chiefs I've worked with: thanks.
To all the Club Vacation gestioners I've worked with: thanks
To all the Club Vacation chiefs of sports I've worked with: thanks
To all the Club Vacation chiefs of animation I've worked with: thanks
To all the Club Vacation chiefs of bars I've worked with: thanks.
To all the Club Vacation organizers I've worked with: thanks.
To all the Club Vacation office staff around the international world: thanks.

As It Unfolds

The story is true and is based on not one but three individuals. They're meeting a group of unique individuals from different parts of the globe in a resort different from all others. The story unfolds when one of them meets a most unusual character named Yoann. That will set in motion an event that shakes the foundation of Louise's heart and gives Andrea something else, much to her surprise. Louise's curiosity pushes her to gravitate to the young man, forsaking all others. This is their story, and it will unfold before your eyes. It begins on a hot August night in New York City.

ONE

A hot August night

*I*t was a late August night, and I could feel the heat of the night as I lay twisting and turning in my bed, seeking comfort. The bedroom window was open, and like always, I'd forgotten to turn off the television in my room. Why? Because sometimes I honestly believed that this damned television helped me fall asleep at nights, especially after being frustrated from working late nights at the Quick Rap Restaurant in downtown New York City.

I knew I needed a vacation after working for two years day in and day out, replacing coworkers, working overtime, and filling in shifts or any changes in schedule. I had a boyfriend but had no idea what love truly was. My first boyfriend's name was Alex. My first sexual experience with him had landed me in the hospital with my legs open for almost two weeks; only my family comforted me. Because of the long wait between us, his sexual urge punished me. I couldn't stop him; he was too strong. I never wanted to see him again, and we broke up that night. As for Alex, he never got the message.

I lay twisting and turning, and there was only one word printed in my mind: *antidote*. That came from a Club Vacation television commercial. I was determined to find out what this antidote was, and I knew it could be found only at Club Vacation.

As I lay dreaming and smiling to myself, I was quickly awoken by the bedroom window, which slammed against the outer side of the house due to a passing breeze. I glimpsed my wristwatch: five minutes before six in the morning. The television sent a weary glow around the still dark room as I lay sleepless and stared in space. I still went over that commercial in my mind. The phrase "antidote, the injection for civilization" never left my mind. Anyone who worked in a big city for two years without some vacation deserved a taste of this so-called paradise.

Thinking about vacation gave me the strength to ease out of bed. The news station went on air for its morning edition. As I walked across the room and looked at the TV, there it was again: the Club Vacation commercial. I couldn't believe all the beauty one place had to offer. I rested my hands upon the television, feeling a bit disappointed I wasn't there at that very moment. I switched it off and hopped back into bed. I slept, dreaming about beaches and sun, until sunshine flooded the room through the opened window and caressed me with its heat.

I heard a knock at my bedroom door. It was my father wondering whether I was working today. It was Sunday, my day off. I jumped out of bed, took a shower, and headed downstairs, looking forward to making myself a jumbo breakfast, which I didn't have time to make on working days. My parents were already seated, enjoying the morning paper. "Good morning," I cheerfully told them. I felt good today.

"Good morning, dear," they both answered softly as I made my way to the fridge.

"Well, I see that at least there is one day in the week you are not working," my father added, noticing I was not dressed in my working uniform.

"No, Father, not this morning."

"Louise, will you then be a part of our church service this morning?" my mother asked in a somewhat disapproving tone. I knew she wanted me to attend all those religious gatherings, but for me, they didn't mean a thing. I wasn't interested one bit in them, plus I had other things on my mind—and even more things to do.

Every Sunday, it was the same story all over again. "Mum, you know how I feel about it all. I do have lots to do today, anyway," I answered while fixing my breakfast.

"I know you work very hard at what you do, but you must put

some time aside for yourself, you know," she answered, still pursuing the subject.

"That's exactly what I'm planning to do, Mother: spend some time on myself for a change," I told her perhaps a bit too impatiently.

"Are you saying you will be leaving us soon?" my father asked with a look of concern on his face.

"No, no, nothing like that. I was planning to take a short vacation away from this fast-moving city life. God knows I need one badly."

Mother gathered her dishes from the table and went to the sink. "Well, that is true. You do need to take a vacation. If you will excuse me, I have to get myself ready for the church service." She made her way to the room.

Father stayed a few minutes more to talk with me. "So when are you planning to leave?" he asked.

"If possible, tomorrow morning. No later than tomorrow evening," I replied while finishing up my breakfast.

"Have you decided where you will be staying? There are a lot of places up north, or on the other side of town," he went on, wondering about my plans.

"No, I want nothing of the sort," I told him, waiting a second or two before going on. "I'm going to one of those Club Vacation villages, where I can see bitches—sorry, Dad—beaches and beautiful weather." I stumbled back on track before continuing on. "Beautiful beaches, beautiful weather. You know—something out of the ordinary, a change from this lifestyle. I'm also planning to ask Andrea to accompany me. You remember her, don't you?" Right then, I had a feeling that because of my mistake, this was not over.

Sure enough, he called me on it. "And about that mistake you made?"

Lying to him, I said, "Just an honest expression for bad men, Dad. Nothing more."

As a man of few words, Dad left it at that, but parents knew their children.

"Well, Dad, like I've said, I'm planning to ask Andrea to accompany me. If she cannot make it, I will travel alone."

With a smirk on his face, Father only looked to me and said, "I'm sure whatever you decide to do is for your own good, Louise. Just be careful, and if ever you need me financially, don't forget I'm here. Well, I'd better get going. Your mother should be ready by now." Father got up from the breakfast table. Sometimes I got the feeling following Mother to church annoyed him.

"Thanks, Dad," I said before he walked away with a slight smile on his face. I thought his acrimonious smile told me something about my white lie, an honest mistake.

I was fond of my father. He was an understandable man who was able to accept anything and anyone. Well, almost anyone, if I excluded some of my old school boyfriends. Mother was a little more reticent to accept matters that were a bit out of the ordinary. She was a very conservative person with a strong tendency toward religion. She was a charming and lovely person willing to speak philosophy with anyone, but anyone else for her was a bit off the wall. Still, they were my parents, and I loved them dearly.

My parents made their way to the church service, but not before wishing me a very good day. Thanks to my father, the news of my leaving traveled fast. Mother knew of my trip and of course didn't agree at all, but my mind was set. Nothing could change it.

After cleaning the breakfast dishes, my first move was to drop a visit to Andrea and convince her about her need for a vacation. I had an hour's drive in front of me because she lived on the other side of town. I took along my best music and pictured my dream vacation.

TWO

My surprise speech to Andrea

Andrea was in her backyard picking flowers from the garden when I entered her driveway. The minute she saw me, she ran toward me with a big smile on her face. "This is quite a surprise! I was not expecting you," she told me.

I got out of my car and smiled back at her. "Well, you know me and the way I like to surprise everyone," I answered as we hugged.

"Yes, you're always full of surprises. What's on your mind this time?" she asked as we stood by the front door.

"Vacation, if you must know."

"Vacation?" she repeated. "Where to, and when do we leave?"

"What do you mean, when do *we* leave?" I replied, feigning surprise.

"Well, isn't that why you're here?" she asked, teasing me as if it was a game we were playing.

"Okay, you win! Tomorrow at the latest. I will try to make the reservation for tomorrow morning," I answered.

"May I also know where we are going?" she asked, anxious to hear about it.

"Sure. Mexico, here we come!"

"Mexico? Wow!"

"Yes, Mexico. That's is if they have a village in that country. I will know only tomorrow after talking with the travel agency."

"Tell me, Louise, who are they?" She did not know much about them.

I just had to say it. "They are none other than the Club Vacation."

"Club Vacation! So we are going big time. I always wanted to see what one of those villages looked like. I hear they have a lot to offer as a vacation resort. Outstanding!"

"I thought you knew nothing about them," I said, grinning.

Andrea pointed her finger at me. "One on you, girl!" We had our own way of speaking sometime. We smiled at each other, and she said, "I think I have one of their brochures in my room. Come on. Let's go inside. May be I can find it." She led the way. "Make yourself comfortable. My parents aren't here; they left to the countryside and will be back tomorrow, hopefully in time to say goodbye."

It didn't take her long to find the brochure, and we dreamed through all those beautiful pages. I couldn't believe the amount of clubs there were. We finally reached the page where they talked about Mexico. It was surprising to find out that Mexico had more clubs than any other country. We had to choose between Guay, Ixt, Playa, or Cancu, one as beautiful as the next. After comparing for what seemed an eternity, we finally agreed on Playa, which was located on the Pacific Coast, 60 miles north of Manzanillo, and 120 miles south of Puerto Vallarta. They had so much to offer, and it was all to our liking: scuba diving, sailing, snorkeling, and tennis. But most of all, what we liked most was the horseback riding.

"Now that we've made our choice inside Tequila Country, I'd better be on my way. We have a lot to do. I will pick you up tomorrow around nine. We'll go at the travel agency and then head directly to the airport," I told her as she accompanied me to the car. "So see you tomorrow, Andrea."

While on the highway, my mind wandered back to Andrea's job. She was my best friend and was such a nice girl. I always admired her. The only difference I could see between us was that my eyes were brown and hers were a pretty blue. We were both slim blondes who stood five feet six inches tall. Our features differed from one another, but many people thought we were sisters. With my high cheekbones and her full lips set in a full square jaw, we made quite a stunning pair.

THREE

My job my decision

After leaving Andrea's place, I headed directly to the Quick Rap Restaurant to let them in on my decision to take a week's vacation. I really didn't expect what was happening to me. I entered the restaurant at three o'clock and didn't leave until after five. Explanation was not enough to save me. I left the restaurant without a job. But nothing was going to stop me from leaving on Monday for Club Vacation. I was determined to get out this city life for a change of scenery. As for my boss, I never really liked her anyway. She could use a change too, starting with her makeup choices. Her high cheekbones could use a different rouge, and her perfume needed a change. If I had not been brought up with decency, I would have told her my thoughts a part of my dark mind.

In a rage, I left the restaurant and drove back home. It was now six forty-five. My parents' car wasn't parked in the driveway; they must still be at their Sunday gathering. In a way, it was good. I had nobody around me to distract me, and God knew I had a lot to do before going to bed.

Four hours later, my suitcases were already set inside my car trunk. I was ready for the journey ahead. Only a few hours more, and paradise would be part of my surroundings. I jumped in bed to get a few hours of sleep. My mind went back to the afternoon at the restaurant. How good would it feel to wrap my hand around the neck of my former boss. That lady really pissed me off. And now I had no job. *Well,* I told myself, *I'll worry about this after my vacation.* And on that thought, I fell asleep.

FOUR

Early rising, Viva Mexico

I woke up early the next morning out of excitement. I got myself ready in no time, and as I entered the kitchen to fix myself some breakfast, I noticed an envelope on the counter addressed to me. I took it in a hurry and put it into my purse, promising myself I'd read it as soon as I had enough time. It was probably my father writing some good news. He'd already left for work, and Mom was still sleeping. I ate in a rush, wrote a goodbye note, and left to pick up Andrea.

It was ten minutes past nine when I parked my car in the driveway at Andrea's place. Her two suitcases were sitting on the front porch, waiting for their destiny. I didn't even have time to press the car horn because Andrea came through the door looking radiant. "Aren't you going to help me out?" she said, smiling. I grinned as I got out of the car in order to give her a helping hand.

"Viva Mexico!" she said, laughing as I picked one of her suitcase. We headed merrily to the car in anticipation of the week in front of us. Suitcases were crammed inside my small trunk, and we exchanged jokes and laughter as we drove away.

I had a flashback to how my mother would sometimes be a jerk. She had her religious ways, and every religious person sought to become perfect. We all sought something, but was it possible to become perfect without the God factor? After all, it was because of the gods that we were all in this messed-up world. That was food for thought.

It took us a while to get into town. The morning traffic was a killer, and Andrea lived on the outskirts of New York City. At twenty minutes past ten, we entered the travel agency, bought our tickets, and made all the necessary arrangements for a one-week stay in Club Vacation's village at Playa. The reservation was confirmed, and we had a flight on Aero Mexico for noon. The lady at the agency was very cooperative and pleasant. Andrea asked her if all of the club workers were that pleasant. The lady made it quite clear to us that she wasn't one of the club's workers, but she did sell tickets and make reservations for them, just like any other travel agency.

The trip and the stay in the village came to eight hundred dollars each. That was called a package deal, and it was worthwhile and to our utmost satisfaction. We asked the lady about a two-week stay, but because we were not sure how long we wanted to stay, the travel agency suggested that if we needed extra days on our vacation, we could make arrangements inside the village. That suited us.

FIVE

At the Airport, the involvement

We left the travel agent in a hurry because time was ticking. We drove directly to La Guardia International Airport and lost precious time trying to find a parking space. It was fifteen past eleven when I looked at my watch. Before getting out of the car, I took Andrea's ticket out of her hand and instructed her to take care of the luggage while I checked us in at the counter. I headed quickly toward the building. At the entrance, I ran into a porter, sent him to poor Andrea, and then rapidly moved on, looking for the counter of Aero Mexico. I finally spotted it and arrived at the counter a bit out of breath. The clerk stared at me with a slight smile playing on his lips, waiting for me to recuperate. While handing him the ticket, I noticed the time on his watch: a little past eleven thirty. *Oh, my God!* I thought to myself. I turned around to see if Andrea was here, but she was nowhere in sight.

"Excuse me, madam," he said in order to gain my attention.

"Oh, I'm sorry. What is it?" I asked while taking a deep breath.

"This flight is leaving ten minutes before its time. They are now making the last announcement. You must hurry to check your luggage, if you want to board this plane," he said matter-of-factly.

I turned around to look for Andrea again, and she arrived with the porter, taking her sweet time. "Andrea, come on!" I shouted at the top of my voice. Everybody standing around me turned to stare at me. I turned back around and stared at the ticket agent, but he was staring at Andrea. I could only think what one of the others in line cried out at me: "Bimbo." Yes, that was what they call us blondes, but some of us were very smart. In relationships, most of us blondes stinks aren't good, but we're getting better at them.

"Is your name on your luggage?" the clerk asked, almost looking me over. I told him everything was tagged without knowing whether anything was tagged. "Well, I advise you to go meet your friend and head directly to immigration at Gate C-24 in order to board the plane on time. Be sure to tell the porter to bring the luggage here now." He didn't have to tell me twice. Besides, I was blonde, and we blondes got preferential treatment.

In no time, I was in front of Andrea, told her about the situation, gave all my loose change to the porter before directing him to the check-in counter.

We ran the length of the airport toward Gate C-24, passed through immigration, and barely made it in time. When we arrived near the entrance of the plane, an agent awaited us, hurrying with our boarding passes and rushing us into the plane. The door was then closed, and like always, the men inside gobbled up the chance of having sexy blondes sit beside them, but we were already given seats according to the boarding passes.

It took us a while to cool ourselves down. We were comfortably seated and chatting, not really believing that all of this was happening. The plane started rolling to take flight on the runway. The move made my purse slip to the floor. I then remembered the letter from my father, so I reached into my purse for it and tore it open. Andrea watched me and said, "Louise, what's this big smile all about?"

Wondering what was in the letter, I kept reading. "Oh, la-la, take a look at this! My daddy left me with a bon voyage note this morning. I had no idea he would go to this extent. He left me a few hundred dollars for personal expenses."

"That's very nice of him," she told me.

At that moment, the stewardess came up to us with a plate of food.

The trip was a very smooth one. Nothing much happened on airplanes anyway. We were much too excited to sleep and had plenty of subjects to talk about. As I looked around, there was a guy sitting one row to the right of us wearing a Club Vacation T-shirt, and I had to smile. By the looks of things, he didn't look too pleased. It was easy to tell why. His girlfriend had all the mouth, and he just sat and obeyed. I could tell she was the moneymaker, and I was sorry for not minding my own business. At one point, our eyes made contact, and he wanted to smile back but couldn't. A man could only take so much of not being in charge of his relationship; sooner or later, the relationship would be over. I decided to sit here, mind my business, and enjoy the plane ride; I hoped he would too. Finally, three hours later, we landed at the airport in Puerto Vallarta.

Six

The disembarkment

*A*fter the plane came to a full stop, we were told to disembark onto the runway, and we had to walk into the building. What a difference this airport was compared to the one we'd left in New York. It was so small! There were no facilities to take the passengers from the plane to the building. When I saw the face Andrea made, I burst out laughing. She could be so funny when she wanted to be.

We went through customs and immigration like butter in a hot pan, no problems at all. As women, there was something special about seeing a man in a uniform; it turned a woman's head, and it even turned on some. I told Andrea, "Leave that one alone. Come on."

We'd heard so many stories about immigration in Mexico being very difficult, but in no time we found ourselves in the lobby and looking around for the Club Vacation representative who was to meet us. He wasn't hard to locate with his T-shirt design, which had a big fork on its front, the symbol of Club Vacation. We walked up to him, and I believed our blonde hair said the rest. "Club Vacation welcomes you to Mexico!" he told us cheerfully while looking at us in a charming way.

He led the way toward what would be our transportation for the next two and a half hours. To our surprise, it was a bus similar to a Greyhound, but it had Pacifico written on it. We had expected a beaten old bus, but to our relief it was very comfortable, with refreshments served. It was already five o'clock when we boarded the bus. There were plenty of unoccupied seats because we were only eleven passengers headed to the club. We settled ourselves in the front seat. I didn't want to miss anything along the trip, unlike Andrea, whose first interest was in the male specimens. On a trip like this, that was my second interest.

We blondes held a secret—or should I say, all women held some kind of mental secret. Let me explain. I had always been in love with a male image in my head. My thoughts saw him as a perfect specimen of a man: tall, built, handsome, in shape, perfect, black hair, beautiful lips, tanned skin, and a sweet smell. When we went out in public, all eyes were intrigued with him. Damn it! It took me five years to understand he had not spoken to me once in five years. I was a fool to neglect so many others because of him. Was I wrong?

Reality was real, and so were the men, but not that perfect man in most women's minds. He was a fool who couldn't even speak for himself without help. On his own, he couldn't even ask, "How was your day?" I suffered because of that, but at least now I got to make a choice. He was no more important to me than his image, which had long ago left me.

As we sat staring out the window, the representative called out for our attention. "Please excuse me," he said with a foreign accent. "Let me present myself. My name is Mark, and welcome once again to Mexico! I am in charge of traffic. If any of you have any problems concerning your flight arrangements, don't hesitate to see me at the village. As you may already know, we have a trip of two and a half hours before reaching the club, so please relax and make yourselves comfortable. I have refreshments here if you care for some. Your rooms will be given to you at the village. On behalf of our chief of the village, Lawrence, welcome to Mexico!"

Everyone applauded with excitement, and some whistled. We were then on our way. It took us ten minutes to reach the only local village we'd cross on our trip. It was a very touristy place, given all the many hotel buildings. It was the village of Puerto Vallarta, a lovely little place on the coast. The road took us higher and higher into the mountains. My eyes opened up to such great beauty, with mountaintops buried in the clouds, green land spread out as far as the eyes could see, and fresh air that was so different from what I was used to. This was a land which humankind had forgotten—nature at its best.

Time moved on as we passed mountains, land, and rivers. Two and a half hours later, the bus finally slowed down, and I could see a big sign for Club Vacation Playa directly in front of us. I couldn't wait to see it. We drove on until we reached a gate, where security guards let us in. *The club provides its visitors proper security,* I thought to myself, and it made me feel secure yet free at the same time. I remembered I had to change my watch to compensate for the time difference in Mexico. With a time difference of two hours, it was now 5:30 p.m. in Mexico. On our way to the parking lot, we came across lovely gardens blossoming with bougainvillea rich with all different colors, and there were so many tennis courts that it was incredible. On our left, we could see a ranch where people were busy getting themselves ready for a horseback riding excursion. We heard music drifting over us, and after turning a corner, there were about fifty people, mostly young, clapping and waving to us in a welcoming fashion and singing a song we would probably learn as the days went by.

SEVEN

The arrival, the information, the satisfaction

Andrea and I looked at each other in amazement, and at this minute we didn't regret having spent all that money to get here. We were enchanted. It was quite a sight to see all those young, beautiful, tanned people dressed with colorful pieces of cloth draped around their bodies in so many different ways. As we got off the bus, they welcomed us warmly and led us to a small outside amphitheater where more beautiful people awaited us with cocktails and invited us to take a seat.

As we sat down, Andrea looked at me. "Louise, don't you think this place has a beautiful Roman look to it?"

"Yes," I said, impressed by the sight. "And maybe a touch of the Aztecs. I remember reading about them in my history courses."

At that moment, loud music started, and the beautiful hosts sang and made all sorts of gestures to the music. "Good afternoon, ladies and gentlemen," one of them said on a microphone. He was tall with brown hair, and he spoke with a French accent. "My name is Lawrence, chief of this village, and on behalf of my GS team, we welcome you to Playa, the land of sea, sun, and tequila. Your rooms will be given to you by Sara and Janet here, in the far right corner." At that, two girls stood up so people could see them. "Then the GS will help you find your rooms. The time in Playa is five forty-five, and I expect to see you all here once again for a brief informational meeting at seven o' clock so you can get better acquainted with all the actives offered in the village. Once again, welcome, and have a nice stay."

Everything was well organized, and we had our assigned rooms in no time at all. Two good-looking hosts offered to lead the way to our rooms. We were allocated a room on the left side of the village, near the boutique. We could hardly take in all the beauty that surrounded us. *This really is the antidote for civilization,* I thought to myself. It was a paradise.

I looked at Andrea and knew she had something on her mind. "These people do have a nick for gardens. So beautiful!" she cried out. I shook my head, struck dumb for words. She'd said it all.

Our room faced the ocean, and all I could think was, *Bikini beach, here we come.* Andrea looked at me and smiled. We were thinking the same thing. A nice breeze drifted through the screened windows when I entered the porch that adjoined the front of the room. I was so curious to see the room that I left Andrea and the two hosts on the doorstep and entered. The room by itself was furnished with two twin beds and a walled-in night table. An air-conditioning unit placed under the window, but with the breeze coming in, it was unnecessary to turn it on. I opened the door to the bathroom to find a nice shower decorated in Mexican fashion.

"Where are you, Louise?" Andrea said upon coming in.

"I'm in the bathroom," I called out. "Isn't this place marvelous?"

"It really is," she said while looking around the place. "Do you believe it? We already have an invitation to share a table tonight at dinner! His name is Paul, and he is really late! He works here and teaches sailing."

"Well, you sure don't lose time!" I told her, and we both laughed.

"I think I'm going to do a bit of sailing during my stay," she said excitedly, and we laughed again. "Have you seen this view we have of the ocean?" she went on. "We can also see most of the village from here too. This is so beautiful. I'm so glad we came. Aren't you?"

"You'd better believe it, my dear. The beach is gorgeous, and the water sparkling like a million little lights is so inviting."

Our reverie was cut short by a knock on the door. It was a worker bringing our suitcases.

"I think I need to take a swim, and fast. What about you, Andrea?"

"You don't have to ask twice, Lou-Lou!" she replied.

EIGHT

Bikini beach, I am yours

t took us a few minutes to rummage through our luggage to find our bikinis, change, and head down to the beach. We met a lot of vacationers on our way, and everyone greeted one another warmly. While walking along, I said to myself, *Bikini beach, I am yours.* Finally, here we were, walking with our blonde hair blowing in the wind. That alone was enough to die for after coming from New York City. At last, I had the pleasure of sinking my feet into the shining white sand. I even bent down to grab a handful of that exquisite softness.

"Look at all the people. There must be at least two hundred people here," Andrea said, also reaching down for a feel of the beautiful sand.

The slight breeze felt so good on my skin. As we lazily walked toward the water's edge, I took in all the beauty in front of me: the beautiful blue sky, laced with only a few puffs of clouds; the sailboats on the horizon; and especially all the greenery surrounding the beach. I was dazed enough to forget I was walking with Andrea. It was only when she shoved me in the ribs that I acknowledged her.

"Come on, Louise! The water is so warm. It feels great!" she shouted as she ran into the water, splashing and throwing water at me.

"Don't forget the meeting at seven!" I shouted before continuing with my walk. I was enthralled by the hills and mountains that surrounded Playa. It seemed like a dormant giant protecting what was once his.

As I stood there looking up at the hills, I felt a sudden tap twice on my left shoulder. For a minute I thought it was Andrea, but as I turned around, I saw an elderly, bald-headed man in a nice little red swimsuit looking at me. He couldn't have been more than five feet tall and was in his late forties. "Good evening," he said in a calm voice as a slight smile came to his lips. "I see you're also looking up at those mountains. Isn't it amazing how they seem to wrap themselves around the village?"

"Oh, yes, it is amazing," I replied, trying to figure out his accent.

"I come out here every afternoon," he went on, "just to look at them and see how they seem to come down into the sea. It makes the village look like it could never escape, which is why we must come to it. Please excuse me for not introducing myself. My name is Vladimir, and I'm from Germany," he said, reaching out to shake my hand.

"Louise, from New York City, and I'm very happy to meet you. Why so far from home?" I asked him while giving him a quick handshake.

"Because I love visiting the Club Vacation locations, where I can meet American people for a change. I have visited seven clubs in Europe. This is my first one out of Europe," he admitted.

"This is my first experiment with the club, and I'm already enjoying it."

"I am sure you will. Well, I must get going. I'm part of the beer-drinking contest taking place at seven thirty. I'm sure we'll meet again," he said as he shook my hand once again before leaving.

As if on one cue, Andrea was at my side. "Who was the man you were talking to?" she asked curiously.

"He looks like a professor. He's from Germany, but I don't really know what he does in life. We didn't speak of that subject. He was telling me he's visited seven Club Vacation locations, and how this one's beauty amazed him." We talked while walking back to our room, greeting so many people along the way.

It was six thirty-five when I took a quick glimpse at my watch. Andrea went directly to the shower while I ironed my dress for the night. We had to make it fast in order to be able to attend the seven o'clock meeting. I took my shower, and unbelievable as it was for us, we were out of the room and heading for the small amphitheater at five minutes to seven. We didn't know our way around, but fortunately a nice GS helped us out by accompanying us. We had to get acquainted with our surroundings soon, but all would be done in its own good time. At the entrance of the amphitheater, one of the smiling hostesses handed us a small booklet, which we learned to call the Club Vacation passport. I remembered a few of the faces from the bus trip, and we watched everyone waiting for the scheduled meeting to begin.

The chief of the village made his appearance after we took a seat. He looked stunning in a silver suit, seemed self-confident, and had a warm smile.

"Ladies and gentlemen, good evening, and once again welcome. We planned this informational meeting for you so you can fully understand what the club has to offer you throughout your vacation." He went on talking, telling a few jokes to relax his audience. He was very funny as he explained the Club Vacation way of living. "Remember that when you come to Club Vacation's villages, you are stepping out of your world and into ours. As an example, money does not exist in the club. Never will you have to put your hand into your pocket. Instead, you will have to sign for all your purchases to your room number and pay for them only at the end of your stay. This is also true at the bar, where you acquire bar beads at the hostess desk that are also connected to your room number. These beads, which can connect and be used as necklaces, can be exchange for any drink at the bar, We also have a boutique for your shopping spree and a bazaar for any last-minute needs."

The meeting lasted twenty minutes. Each chief of service came to explain the activities they were in charge of, from horseback riding to excursions throughout fascinating ancient cities and villages; to land sports such as volleyball, basketball, and tennis; to water sports like sailing, snorkeling, and scuba diving in the most beautiful underwater world. The meeting was concluded by a guided tour of the village: the beach, the disco, the restaurant, the arts and crafts workshop, and all the accommodations offices (such as the planning or traffic office for rooms or flight problems, as well as a hostess desk and stage theater for night shows).

There was even an area to enjoy classical music and one for cycling. The chief of sports had everyone's curiosity aroused when he talked about special picnic trips scheduled on Tuesday mornings. The Club Vacation passport contained all information pertaining to any activities and dining hours, and it included a small map of the village. I was glad to have attended the meeting, and so was Andrea, because now we were familiar with our surroundings.

Before splitting up from the group, I had to ask a question of the chief of sports, who was now finishing his tour. "Can you tell me what is the meaning of GS and GG?"

"The club has recruited young people from all over the world, and because they all shared the same happiness, kindness, and gentleness, they were all called GS, which stands for 'gentle staff.' Everyone coming here on vacation also shares that same happiness, kindness, and gentleness, so they are called GG, or 'gentle guest.' Are there any more questions I can answer for you?"

"Thank you. I don't have any more questions," I answered.

"For your information," he went on, "we will be having the continuation of our Olympic day with a beer-drinking contest at seven thirty, followed by an Italian buffet dinner at eight. And be sure you don't miss the GG show at the big amphitheater at ten tonight, followed by a bonfire with music on the beach at eleven thirty. For the late bird, the disco will open its doors at midnight. I wish you all a nice stay." He gave a smile, and then we guests scattered in different directions.

Andrea and I headed directly for the hostess desk to buy our first bag of bar beads. Then we walked to the adjoining bar to order our first drinks. "Here is to our first vacation in paradise," I toasted as I touched glasses with Andrea.

"I'll drink to that! Oh, look! There's Paul, the sailing instructor, coming our way. Don't you think he's gorgeous? Look at him. So tall and lean!"

"Well, my dear, this time I agree 100 percent," I answered her, thinking how different it was here for blondes. After looking around at so many of the other vacationers, I got the picture. Here, preference for blondes lost its merit because of the amount of outstanding men and European women who were slim and tall, making them look like models. We seemed like a second class.

Andrea and I usually didn't have the same taste in men, but this time I agreed that this guy was really good looking. His face was deeply tanned, and his deep blue eyes looked like little lights brightening up his smiling face. His high cheekbones were framed by sun-bleached fine hair. He really did honor his European heritage, and he was fine. After seeing Andrea waving out to him, he came our way. "Hello there, ladies. You look sensational," he said, letting his eyes roam a little longer in Andrea's direction.

"Louise, this is Paul. Paul, this is Louise, my best friend," Andrea said.

"Pleased to meet you, Paul. Andrea told me a lot about you," I said winking at Andrea before placing my bar beads together.

"I hope it was all good things," he said with a grin. At that moment music came from the small outside amphitheater near the bar.

"I wonder what the music is for?" I said, looking in Paul's direction.

"The beer-drinking contest is starting now. The white team is against the red team. I should be heading for the dance floor in the amphitheater. Why don't you join the crowd and see what it's all about? You'll have a lot of fun. I'll meet you here around eight for dinner, okay? See you later." Then he was on his way to watch the contest.

We took our exotic pina coladas and made our way toward the beer-drinking contest. The place was crowded with cheering people. I spotted my afternoon encounter, Vladimir, preparing for the contest against his opponent, who was almost twice his size. Andrea noticed my big smile and looked in the same direction.

"Hey, look, it's Vladimir, the German I met earlier this afternoon," I told her. "Don't you think they look like David and Goliath? That man is twice his size." I pulled her along to get a better view.

"You're right, it does look a little funny. Let's see who wins this one. I bet the big guy can really gulp that beer fast," she said.

There was a lot of excitement in the air. The host of the contest asked the audience for quiet in order for both men to be able to concentrate better. He then went on to explain the rules of the contest, asking both men to begin by resting their hands flat on the table. The cheering now stood quiet for the final countdown.

The host went on. "Are you ready, guys? Three, two, one—go!" Vladimir's hands were a fraction of a second faster than his opponents, who were struggling with the yellow liquid like two drowning fish. The crowd started cheering the two opponents. In no time, Vladimir had gulped down his two mugs of beer and was declared the winner. We couldn't believe it. We had never seen such a short man drink beer so quickly! He and his teammates jumped up and down in excitement at his victory. Vladimir received more kisses from his team than he'd probably ever had in his entire life. We applauded wildly, and when he looked in my direction, I winked my congratulations to him. He smiled back at me and then returned his attention toward his team. He was in for a medal now, and he loved it.

It was wonderful to feel all the warmth and happiness surrounding us. It seemed as though we were one big family gathered here for a summer picnic. Andrea showed me a thumb's-up.

NINE

Dinner and the after math

*W*e mingled with the crowd, met a few people, and enjoyed the contest until eight o'clock. Andrea grabbed my arm and pulled me toward the bar because she didn't want to miss her dinner date with Paul. I could see Paul's face through the crowd, trying to locate us. As we made our way to the bar, I could see the smile Andrea reserved for Paul. He went at Andrea with a twinkle of politeness in his eyes.

"Well, I don't know about you guys, but I am starving!" I said, smiling. "How about attacking that Italian buffet? I can't wait to sink my teeth into one of those pizzas."

"Sure, let's go. I'm starving too," Paul said as he led the way to the entrance of the restaurant right above us.

People were in line at the entrance of the restaurant. We squeezed in and went upstairs with the flow of the crowd. On each step, there were workers lined up and dressed in beautiful costumes. The sight was breathtaking. The line ended up at the top of the stairs, where the chief of the village greeted each GG with a handshake and a smile.

Once we entered, we were stunned to see the amount of food. I'd forgotten it was a self-service buffet dinner until Paul kindly reminded me by placing a plate in my hand. I strolled from buffet to buffet, admiring and fascinated by the options. The pizza buffet had so many different types that it was like a dream. There was so much to choose from that I didn't know what to take. I tried to fit a little of everything on my plate. Then I accidentally bumped into a man in front of me, who turned around with a quizzical expression. I greeted him with my best smile.

He looked at me, smiled, looked at my stuffed plate, and then glanced back at me, "Is that all for you?" he said rather seriously, pointing at my plate.

"Uh, no. This is for my girlfriend and me," I said, embarrassed. I rapidly searched behind me for Andrea, who was nowhere in sight. After looking for Paul and Andrea, I caught up with her at the last buffet. "Are you ready to find a seat?" I asked her.

"Yeah," Paul said, following us. "I was looking for you two."

Andrea stated, "I was looking at the pizza buffet."

"What else?" I said, laughing.

Paul went directly to one of the dinner hostesses so that we could be placed together. The hostesses were choosing seats for everyone in the restaurant. Each table could seat eight people total so guests always had new faces to dine with. It was an easy and relaxed way to meet one another. After we were seated, we introduced ourselves to three friendly, smiling Mexicans who spoke very little English, as well as a French couple on their honeymoon.

The food was excellent and the wine warmed our spirits. After devouring everything on my plate, I stood up, excused myself from the table, and came back with a plate full of exotic fruits. Paul looked concerned when he saw my collection. "Louise, I suggest you not to eat that fruit yet. There is some delicious dessert on its way to the table"

"But I thought it was a self-service dinner?"

"Well, you're probably right."

"I'll wait a while and see what's coming," I said, smiling back at him and setting aside my plate.

"Andrea was telling me it was your first time in the club, and so far she likes it very much. How about you?" he asked as he filled my glass with wine.

"From what I have seen so far, I find it very interesting. It definitely is the antidote injection for civilization that I needed! This is what they advertise for the club back at home, and thanks to those enticing commercials, here we are. I'm so glad we made the decision."

As Andrea came back with a second helping of pizza, a waiter placed a rich chocolate cake in the center of the table—Andrea's favorite. "Well, I guess I'll pass on my pizza. You should have told me there was a desert like this coming our way!" she joked, nudging Paul in the ribs.

"You were already gone when I told the table about it," he answered her, putting his arm around her in a brotherly way. Paul reached for the cake and placed it in front of the honeymooners, and they loved it. Smiles filled the table. Then Paul raised his glass and made a special toast, wishing them a happy honeymoon in the club and a long life together. We all raised our glasses and toasted to long life. We blondes found honeymoons touching, and we could only smile away our tears.

A few hours later, the three of us were back at the bar. This was when I noticed that all the GS were dressed in red and white. I guessed it was to match the teams colors for the Olympic day. "How about a coffee, girls?" Paul said, breaking in on my thoughts.

I said, "I'll pass on the coffee, but I would be glad to get my hands on a Grand Marnier. I need it after that big dinner."

"And I would be more than pleased with a cognac," Andrea replied, feeling her stomach.

I reached into my pocket to fetch my bar beads and placed them on the bar as Paul ordered the drinks. "That's okay, I'll pay for them," he said as he took my beads and put them back in my hand.

"You don't have to feel obliged, you know. You've already been more than nice to us. Maybe we should be buying you a drink," I said, smiling.

"It's my pleasure. Believe me," he said, smiling back at us.

"Tell me something, Paul. I see all those people around here seem to know each other. When did they all come into the village?" I asked him curiously.

"Well, most of the GGs are on Saturday and Sundays, but throughout the week, small groups do come in, mostly what we call village-village, meaning people who book only a short stay in two or more club at a time, they also arrange their own arrival and departure and their own transportation. Most of the guests got here two days ago, and with the Olympic day, it's an easy way to get to know each other."

"I see. Where do most of them come from?" I asked while he quickly paid the bartender and handed us our drinks.

"Mostly from California because it is so close, but we do have people from all over the world," he said, smiling.

Andrea was intent on his every word while gently sipping her cognac. "Tell me a little bit more about this Olympic day, Paul," she said sweetly.

"It's a day of many different games played against two teams, the red and the white, where people can have a good time while getting to know each other. That's mainly what it is. It's really a very interesting day. It starts on the beach at ten in the morning with an egg-throwing contest, followed by tug-of-war and jumping bag contests. Throughout the day, there are events such as basketball, volleyball, water polo, and even a swimming contest. Trivial pursuit is one of the games, and you saw the beer-drinking contest already. The Olympic day is concluded by a show performed by the GGs. I tell you, if there were more than twenty-four hours in a day, we would still be going on, but every good thing has an end."

We went on talking and sipping our drinks. All the while, more GSs came to the bar, and Paul introduced us to them. The atmosphere was great; it was like being among good friends. Music drifted to us from the dance floor of the small amphitheater. A quiet glimpse at my watch told me it was nine twenty-five.

Upon seeing the direction of my gaze, Paul said, "This music signals the beginning of the dancing on the floor. It usually last a half hour and is right before the night shows. It's funny, and more so after a big dinner! Burns the calories."

At that moment, a tall brunette with curly hair approached him, almost throwing herself on him. It was obvious she'd had a bit too much to drink. Andrea and I looked at each other, smiling at the situation. "Let's see what this dancing is all about," Andrea whispered to me. We excused ourselves to Paul to settle his own affairs. The dance floor was already filled up by GSs. It made it very easy to walk up and start dancing. In no time, we had more men approaching us than we could cope with. All of them wanted to be friendly and introduced us to more people until we found ourselves among a large group of people. I wondered whether it was because of us being blonde, but it sure felt different in this kind of atmosphere.

Around ten, the host picked up the microphone. "Ladies and gentlemen, it is now showtime!" At that moment, the disco music dimmed and was replaced by an instrumental opening song. Everyone scattered off the dance floor and headed for the stage theater to find a good seat to view the night show.

We followed the crowd, but as I looked back to make sure Andrea was still following me, I saw that she was nowhere in sight. There were so many people that it was hard to spot her. I continued though with the crowd when all of a sudden, I was pulled by the arm. It was Andrea followed by Andrew and David, two of the first guys we had met on the dance floor. "There you are. They invited us to sit with them for the show," Andrea said.

"Oh, good. It's fine with me," I replied, smiling at them.

"Good. I like to be sitting up high, so let's go in the back," David suggested as he led the way through the crowd to the back of the amphitheater.

We found very good seats just as the light dimmed to darkness, and the chief of the village came out from behind the stage curtain, clapping his hands. The audience followed his example in cheers. I imagined how important this show was to friends and relatives of those who were performing tonight. The music dimmed to let the chief of the village make his opening speech, and then the show began. It was very funny because the performers were all guests and had had only three hours of practice. There were confusion and laughter, and some did on-the-spot improvisation. It was hilarious. The costumes were a show by themselves, so beautiful and colorful.

At the end of the show, David whispered into Andrea's ear, "You will like what is coming up next. They're called the crazy signs. They're really great and crazy at the same time!" He smiled.

"What are the crazy signs?" she asked.

At that moment, the lights came on, and the chief of the village asked the audience to stand. He was then joined by all the GSs on stage and all the GGs who had performed. They started doing the crazy signs to music. Andrea and I tried our best to follow, but there were so many of those signs to remember that we had a hard time keeping up. David and Andrea were doing well, but they still missed a few. There were a few more sing-alongs, which we found very amusing, and then the chief of the village thanked the performers by inviting them to a few drinks at the bar, gifting the captains of the red and white teams with a beautiful printed pareu. He went on to remind the people of the picnic at ten the next morning. After bade good night, we heard the music start again on the dance floor.

I felt full of energy and had nothing else in my mind but to dance the night away. I made my way to the dance floor, thinking Andrea was following me, but instead it turned out to be Andrew. He seemed a very nice guy and had light brown hair with eyes that matched the color of his thin, smiling mouth. He was at least six feet two inches tall, but he was not my type of man, especially not with the lingering sent of beer on his mouth.

We danced for a while, and then I excused myself, using the ladies' room as an escape from him. I then headed directly to the main bar to refuel on a pina colada and saw Andrea and David. It looked like Andrea was having a really good time.

"So where is my buddy?" David asked me as he looked me over.

"On the dance floor having a good time," I replied coolly.

"Yeah, well, I'm sure he can take care of himself now! Would you like something to drink?" he asked.

"A pina colada, please."

"What would you say if we joined in for the bonfire on the beach later?" Andrea asked me while David ordered my drink.

"I don't know. I am a bit tired considering the day we've had. Plus, I would like to wake up early tomorrow to check out the scuba diving," I replied.

"Are we going to the picnic tomorrow morning?" she asked eagerly.

"Why don't we both wait until tomorrow comes to see how we feel?" I suggested as David handed me my drink. I could see he was also eager to know whether we would be going. "If you all will excuse me, I'm going to sit by the pool for a while. Thanks for the drink, David. I'll see you later." I went toward the pool, which was situated about two hundred feet from the bar. Everything seemed to be situated around the bar.

The night was beautiful, and the sky shone with millions of stars. I sat on the edge of the pool, letting my feet lazily soak in the warm water. I thought about what a luxurious life this place offered, and it was so peaceful. I wondered what it would feel like to have this kind of life all the time.

At that moment, Andrea startled me by sneaking up next to me. "Well, shall we go see what this bonfire is all about?" she said with a bright smile.

"Where is David? Isn't he with you?"

"No, he was talking with someone, so I slipped away."

We walked lazily along until we reached the beach where the bonfire was about to be lit. In no time, flames roared almost as if to lick the sky, and sing-along music flowed toward us. There were people spread out around the big fire singing, drinking, and even dancing to the slow music. Others relaxed on the sand.

The fire lasted about an hour before it was down to almost nothing. By then, Andrea and I had thrown so much sand onto each other that we decided to join the group of people taking a late-night swim in the ocean. In laughter, we headed back to our room. After showering, Andrea fell asleep as soon as her head hit the pillow. I went through the Club Vacation passport a while before dozing.

TEN

Early rising

At seven thirty, my eyes opened as if on cue. It seemed it would take a while to shake off the old routine. In no time, I was washed, dressed, and ready for action. Andrea was still snoring away, so I silently made my way out of the room to browse the village before getting myself some breakfast. The eight o'clock sun felt so good, and the sky was true blue, unspoiled by clouds. It promised to be a very beautiful day.

I went by the club's boutique, and the window displays convinced me I had to come back during opening hours. The clothes looked fantastic. *Wait till Andrea sees this,* I thought. I continued my tour and came up to the arts and crafts shop, where silk painting and jewelry making were done. I looked through the window and saw a few of the art-workers and some GGs; some of the displayed work were gorgeous and others were abstract. Now, this was something I would fine interesting. I promised myself to go there later in the day and try out my talent.

I followed the walkway that I thought would lead me to the opposite side of the amphitheater, but instead I found myself entering a large, open, thatch-roofed plaza that featured ping-pong tables, a large universal weight lifting machine, and free weights. My attention immediately focused on the free weights, and I tried them out before continuing my walk. The walkways lead me back to the big stage amphitheater, and at that point I knew how to orient myself. From there, I could find the dining room, and it took me no time at all to climb the stairs because I was starving. I grabbed a plate and toured the buffet, astonished to see so much food for breakfast. There were numerous types of bread: cheese, wheat, raisin, cinnamon, bacon, chocolate, croissants, and sweet milk bread. They were beautiful and fantastic. There were pitchers of creamed chocolate, as well as strawberries, bananas, mangoes, cantaloupe, oranges, papayas, apples, ice-cold milk, and freshly squeezed juices. There were also a hot grill, where eggs, bacon, potatoes, or even ham could be cooked. I noticed yogurts, all different kinds of cheese, hot coffee, hot chocolate, and hot milk. Nothing was missing. All this beautiful food, and I had one little stomach.

That morning, I left the restaurant filled to the limits. I could barely move. All I wanted after breakfast was to get to my room. Andrea was awake when I entered. "Are you okay?" she asked me, wondering why I chose to lie flat out on my bed.

"Oh, I'm all right, just a little too full from eating. I need to rest for a while," I replied, making myself comfortable.

"Tell me what's there for breakfast."

"I don't have enough time to tell you because there is so much! You would miss breakfast by the time I finish, and it would be a shame." I stretched out on my bed as Andrea finished preparing herself for breakfast.

ELEVEN

The challenge, the meeting

W hen I woke again, I looked at my watch, It was already ten minutes to ten! I jumped out of bed and noticed a note on Andrea's bed. She would be at the picnic. I had to rush to make it on time for the scuba diving session. The team was to leave at ten thirty. I quickly got myself together and ran down to the opposite end of the beach to the scuba diving shack. Now, all blondes were pretty with their hair blooming out, but when tied up, sometime it was not so interesting. Mine was tied up in a ponytail and looked bright. I arrived at the shack out of breath.

"Hello, and good morning. Can I help you?" The GS in charge asked me with a lovely French accent.

"I would like to sign up for scuba diving, please," I answered, smiling.

"That's great. Have you ever scuba dived before?" he asked me.

"No, but I'm a very good swimmer."

"I wish that was enough, but it isn't. You will have to take a medical before I can let you scuba. All you have to do is go to the infirmary and see Alex, the doctor. Tell him you came for a scuba test. He'll give you a paper, which you'll bring back to me, and then you are on the road!"

The law is the law, I thought. I set my pace to a jog and left the shack, trying to remember where the infirmary was. According to the map in the Club Vacation passport, It was situated somewhere near the entrance of the village. As I walked toward the entrance of the village, I was lucky enough to come across a GS who showed me to the infirmary and even introduced me to Alex, the doctor.

After explaining my situation, Alex didn't waste any time doing his job. He gave me a full examination, signed the paper, and handed me the form. I thanked him, and in no time I was crossing the village once again. Flying would have been faster, but technology was not that far along yet.

I reached the scuba diving shack again, a little this time out of breath, and handed the form to the same GS. He carefully looked it over and then looked back at me. "Well, Louise, you are on your way. My name is Patrick, and I'm in charge of the scuba department," he said, giving me a quick handshake. "Your equipment is right beside the door, and Sherry will be waiting for you at the end of the dock to give you a mask and fins. Have a nice day!,

I quickly picked up my scuba tank and placed it onto my back. I started walking the sixty feet that separated me from the end of the dock with the heavy tank on my back. I had some good exercise. I wondered how in the world I would not sink right to the bottom of the ocean with that kind of load on my back. It made me a little nervous.

I could see four people already in the water in full diving gear. Sherry handed me a mask, showed me how to adjust it, and gave me fins. She explained that we were only four because everyone else was out on the picnic trip. Sherry was from Los Angeles and was a very beautiful girl. She was about my height with long chestnut brown hair. We talked like we'd known each other for a long time. Another instructor who was already in the water asked her if there were any more people to join them. "Yes one more," Sherry shouted as she looked back at me. I started to get nervous because it was my first time. Sherry must have guessed how I felt. "Are you ready?" she asked me, looking directly into my eyes. I nodded with a hesitating smile. "It's gonna be all right! Just remember this all the times: never let yourself panic. It's the only advice I can give you right now. Now, go on, jump—and don't forget to hold your mask."

I said to myself, *Easy for the expert to say.*

I wasn't panicking, but my legs shook like crazy. I finally found the courage to jump and was very surprised to find that the weight of the equipment felt nonexistent. I didn't fall to the bottom like a heavy rock!

I swam a little to join the three others who were facing the instructor. The instructor was a French GS. He gave us the basics about scuba diving, and we descended into the water in pairs. We were working in about twenty feet of water. It was the first time I had set my eyes on the underwater world. I couldn't believe how clear and bright it was. Small fishes of all shapes and beautiful colors moved around us as if we were a part of their world. I had never seen anything like it. It was beautiful beyond words to see the treasures hidden underwater. I saw corals and vegetation mingling together in an array of colors. I even glimpsed a school of seahorses, two starfish, and a wandering ray. I was enthralled by all the wonders that could be found in the midst of nature. My companion quickly brought me back to reality. Time went by so quickly and before we knew it, it was time to set ourselves back to a slow decompression ascent. I knew it was the most dangerous step if made in the wrong way, so I was extremely careful.

A short while later, we were standing on the dock, shaking hands, and introducing ourselves. There were Thomas and Marian from Texas, and Kelly, my scuba diving companion, was also from Texas. They had that wonderful, sweet Southern drawl. Sherry collected our masks and fins while Alain asked for our attention. "I just want you to know you have passed your first test," he said cheerfully. This comment brought smiles to our faces. "I would like to see you all back here at two thirty this afternoon to continue our lesson. If you would please take your tank back to the scuba shack, I would be most grateful. See you all later!"

It was already eleven thirty. I made a quick stop at my room for a change into dry clothes. I wanted to be on time to browse the boutique before it closed at noon. At ten minutes to twelve, I made my way between the racks and admired exotic clothing and jewelry, all signed with the Club Vacation insignia, including the famous heart trident. Ten minutes was not enough time to shop, so I promised myself I'd do some more shopping later.

I headed toward the main bar to get a cold drink. It was a very hot and humid day. The sun was high in the sky, and the altitude was high. The sun's rays were almost unbearable in direct exposure. I couldn't understand how people were able to sunbathe at that time of day.

As I was neared the bar, I heard someone calling my name. I turned around to see two guys sitting on the tops of a bench. They laughed and invited me to join them. One of them was short and slim and looked like an Indian; the other was tall with dark skin, and he had very short hair and a little mustache. They looked like they were having a very good time, and I wondered whether it was at my expense. I made my way to them, wondering how they knew my name because I had never seen them before. "Well, guys, I'm sure you're going to tell me," I said, waiting for their reaction.

"Tell you what?" the short one asked.

"Where we have met. Or haven't we met?"

"Ooo. We know your name, but you don't know ours. You see, news travels fast in this village, and more so when it concerns a beautiful girl like you," the short one replied as he pulled a cigarette out of his front shirt pocket, threw it in the air, and caught it with his mouth.

I thought, *Blonde attention again.*

"Would you have a match?" he asked innocently.

"Sorry, but I don't smoke. I must say, it's a lovely way to make a compliment. Do you all work here?"

I asked. "Yes, madam!" the tall one answered, accompanying his words with a little break dance. I finally broke down and laughed.

"My name is Cenny," the short one said. "I am from Mauritius Island. I work at the bar—actually, I'm the chief of bar." He pulled out his lighter to light his cigarette.

"Mauritius? Where is that?" I asked, having never heard it before.

"It's an island on the east side of South Africa," the tall one answered. "And I'm Derick from Jamaica. I work at the disco bar. I work for Shorty here." As he said it, he jokingly shoved Cenny in the ribs and went on break-dancing around him while Cenny used his kung fu movement to catch him.

I couldn't help but laugh at the odd pair. They stopped as suddenly as they started and broke out laughing like little children. "Listen, guys.

As much as I like being with you, I still have to get myself some food because I'm starving. I'll see you around. Nice meeting you," I said, and then I walked into the restaurant.

At that moment, they started singing, "I love you, I love you, I love you," from the Beatles' "Michelle." It made me turned around and smile at them. A few people started looking at them and then at me. I hurried to the stairway inside the restaurant and tried to mingle with the crowd.

An hour later, I walked out of the restaurant as full as could be. The buffet was another magnificent success. With all the different kinds of fishes, it made it quite difficult to resist the pleasure of tasting a little of everything.

When I walked by the main bar, there they were again, my two funny friends, still fooling around. This time they were singing "Figaro" at the top of their lungs, as if they were mad. I walked over to them with a grin on my face. "What's all this noise for? Are you two planning on going into the singing business? Because you won't make it with all that noise."

The short one replied, "We are practicing our number for tonight's lip-syncing contest. We took a bet with the cooking team, and if we lose, we have to wash dishes all night." As he said it, they looked like a pair of sad little puppies. I burst out laughing and left them to their rehearsal, hearing them "Figaroing" as I made my way to my room.

At one fifteen, I decided to put on my bathing suit, enjoy the ocean a bit, and try for a little tan on my milky colored skin before meeting at the scuba shack for another session of underwater beauty.

I met Vladimir on the beach, and we swam a few strokes together before I left him to lie quietly on a lounge chair in the sun. In no time, I decided to walk to the beach bar because the heat was unbearable, and I had a thirst. I came to a structure that had a thatched roof and wood pillars. It had no walls, so a cool breeze always drifted by from the sea, which was about five hundred feet from the beach. The place was almost empty. The bartender noticed me right away.

"So this is the beach bar. It looks pretty neat," I told him, admiring the place.

"It's also a restaurant at night. Whenever you feel like a change of scenery from the upstairs restaurant, you can sign up for this one at the hostess desk," he said while continuing with his work.

I admired the way he wore his pareu; it made him look like a warrior. His shape was the best I had ever seen. His muscles made him look as solid as a rock. He was a dark-skinned man with hair down to his waist, braided together in one long plait.

"I like the way you're wearing your pareu," I said. "How did you do it?"

"It's three pieces of pareu, one across the chest, one around the waist, and another piece around the hips," he answered as he stepped out of the bar so I could have a look at it.

"I see. Strange. I mean, it's unique, but I see no one else with your tying method. What's your name?" I just had to ask.

"My name is Yoann. What about yours?"

"Louise from New York," I told him, smiling.

"Well, Louise from New York, your accent tells otherwise."

I smiled because he was correct. "I'm originally from Montreal, Canada," I admitted.

"Well, I'm from the Bahamas, Nassau, one of the seven hundred islands under the sun," he said.

"Tell me, are there any Club Vacation locations in the Bahamas?"

"There's one on Paradise Island, which is not far from Nassau, and one on Eleuthera Island. There's one coming in San Salvador," he replied.

"They must be very nice. I heard those islands were beautiful. Have you been there lately?"

"Not lately, but I have seen both. I have to admit they are all different from one another. That makes the beauty of traveling from one club to another even more exciting. Is Playa your first club?" he asked me.

"I have to admit it's my first time at Club Vacation."

"And how do you like it so far?"

"I find it very interesting. I've never met so many nice people in one place," I told him.

"I see you didn't join the others for the picnic trip," he noted.

"Really, my interest was on scuba diving this morning."

"Yes, I know. By the way you dashed through here this morning, I knew you could only be a very sporty person," he replied with a smile, which brought one to my own face.

"I was running to the infirmary for a scuba test, and I was a little late," I explained.

"A friend and I are going for a bite at the restaurant. Would you care to join us?"

"Thanks anyway, but I have already eaten." I looked at my watch. "As a matter of fact, I have five minutes to make my way to the scuba shack for my afternoon session."

"Well, I will see you later," he said, reaching out to shake my hand. "By the way Louise, when did you arrive?"

"Yesterday," I answered.

"Take good care now," he said as he walked away. He seemed so different from the other men, with his six feet two inches of pride. His well-bred manner gave him an air of calmness and wisdom.

As I made my way to the scuba shack, I bumped into, Paul who seemed to be dragged by the same girl who had been all over him yesterday night. "Louise, I thought you were at the picnic," he had time to say. He looked as if he wanted to melt right in front of me, but the girl dragged him away without even a side glance toward me.

"Only Andrea went," I said. I hardly think he heard me because he was already almost out of sight.

I hurried to the scuba shack. When I reached it, Alain was there to greet me with a big smile. I could see he had eyes only for me. Everyone was almost ready with their tanks, and they were walking to the end of the dock. Alain offered me some help with my equipment, and then we followed the others and boarded the boat.

The boat ride lasted fifteen minutes. It brought us to a secluded little bay, and once again I was part of the most fascinating world I had ever seen. More fishes, more corals, and more beauty. I wished I could stay among this peacefulness, but of course I was not a fish. After my tank was empty, up I'd go, back to my own world. This time we stayed about an hour in the water. Alain had his job to do, so he did not spend as much time as he would have liked with me, but I already had my partner in Kelly. We boarded the boat for the return trip.

Once back at the scuba shack, after my equipment was stored, Alain approached me. "Louise, how did you like your dive?"

"It was wonderful. I enjoyed every minute of it," I answered, smiling.

"I'm glad you're happy. How about having dinner with me tonight?" He busied himself with odd tasks.

"That would be lovely, Alain. How about I meet you at the main bar around eight?"

"I'll be there," he replied eagerly. I left the shack for my room.

On my way through the beach bar, I didn't miss a chance to say hello to Yoann. It was crowded with happy drinking GGs. The last table near the exit was occupied by none other than David and Andrew. They spotted me right away. All blondes were usually friendly, and that was because in Los Angeles and New York, most of us were considered bimbos, but like I said, that was not totally true. At that point, I had no other choice but to walk over to them.

"Louise, there you are. We were expecting you at the picnic," David said in a sleazy voice.

"So how was it?" I asked, but by the looks of their red eyes, I guessed right away they'd been heavily drinking. I wanted to cut this short because I couldn't stand drinking people, and they seemed ready for a good sleep.

"Come here, Louise. Sit down and have a nice little drink with us. You should have seen the picnic. They had so much fuckin' sangria out there, and they made us spin so much around that jug. I'm still dizzy from it all."

"So why don't you go lie down for a while?" I told them, still standing. I was a bit astonished to see them in that fashion.

"It's a secret, but I'll tell you. We promised Devon—that's the bartender at the main bar—that after the picnic, we would still be able to make it to happy hour. We all made a bet on a bottle of champagne," he said, slurring every word.

"Well, I wish you a very good time. I'm going to look for Andrea."
I left without looking back at them.

Andrea was in our room, and I almost bumped into her as I entered.
She was dressed in her aerobic outfit for the class at five o'clock. "There
you are! How was the scuba diving?" she asked me after a hug.

"I don't know how to tell you about it. It was the most beautiful
experience I've had. It's a fascinating world out there," I told her,
noticing the pillow mark on her cheeks. "I see you just woke up. I met
David and Andrew at the beach bar, and they looked ready for a nice
sleep. They were completely bombed out."

Her face lit up at the mention of David's name. "Yeah, I know
what you mean. I thought the crazy signs were pretty crazy, but the
picnic is nothing compared to them. It's much crazier. Game after game
and sangria after sangria until we were all a bit out of it. David drink
so much sangria that he stripped and fell into one of the large barrels
head first. He didn't even know what was happening to him. I drink
a lot too, and when I came back here, all I wanted to do was drop on
my bed like a rock. I woke up about ten minutes ago. What time did
you come in?"

"Oh, maybe around two thirty, or a quarter to three."

"Boy, I can't believe I slept all afternoon! How about joining me
for the aerobics class?" she asked.

"Thanks anyway, but I plan to start on a piece of artwork down
at the arts and crafts shack. I want to try a little silk painting. I'll meet
you back here around seven," I told her while glimpsing my watch. It
was almost five o'clock. "You'd better hurry—you do not want to miss
your class."

"You're right. See you later!" She left for her class.

I went inside the bathroom to change into dry clothes, and in the
mirror I saw the marks left by my bathing suit. *I did get a little suntan,*
I thought as I dressed quickly and headed to the arts and crafts shack.

TWELVE

A touch of silk racing

*I*t was a very nicely decorated workshop, with pieces of silk paintings hanging as exhibits for people to know what wonderful things could be done there, even though not everyone had the talents of professional artists. The place abounded with premade designs that could easily be transferred onto the silk. I knew I was going to enjoy every minute of this.

I met Andrea around seven on the path leading to our room. She looked pooped out but still full of energy. "Louise, let's have a race to the room. Loser pays drinks tonight."

"You've got it!" I answered. I sprinted as if fire was licking my backside. She was not far behind, and just when I felt she was about to reach me, I put everything into it and barely made it to the room, followed by a puffing Andrea. I was also out of breath but proud as any competitor after a victory. Andrea went on to explain she must have blown a gasket and run out of steam. That was enough to make both of us laugh.

Andrea headed directly for the bed, lying flat out like a dead lizard. I hopped into the shower, looking forward to the dinner with Alain. When I got out of the shower, Andrea was in the same position. "Hey, Andrea. You think you gonna make it?" I teased.

She laughed a little. "I sure hope so," she answered, trying to raise herself on her elbows. "I think it was a little too much of that jazz class after the hour of aerobics. The teacher is pretty rough on his exercises."

"If you plan on going tomorrow, maybe I will join you," I said, smiling.

"I'll tell you tomorrow! For now, I don't want to hear the word *exercise*!"

I said to myself, *She's had enough.*

She hopped into the shower, and after a bit of pampering, we were ready to hit the action around a quarter to eight. As we made our way to the main bar, I let her in on my dinner invitation with my French scuba diving instructor. I couldn't tell her much about him because we'd talked so little during the lesson and I'd left him right after, but I promised to keep her informed on any new developments.

THIRTEEN

Meeting Cenny, Derek and Alain again

The bar wasn't as crowed as yesterday, and I wondered where all the people were. Andrea told me she was planning on dining with David and Andrew. *That's if they are still alive after all that drinking,* I thought. Just as we reached the bar, I heard my name being called from the corner. It was Alain, already sipping a pastis while waiting for me. We walked toward him.

"Hello, Alain. How's life?" I asked him with a smile. "I would like you to meet my girlfriend, Andrea. Andrea, this is Alain."

"I am delighted to meet you," Alain told her, and they shook hands.

"Same here," Andrea replied.

"Well, where is everybody tonight?" I asked him.

"Most of them are in the amphitheater watching the video of yesterday's GGs show. Would you like to have something to drink?"

Suddenly someone else said, "Louise, baby, how are you doing? "For a minute I thought to myself; that man could ruin a good thing. I turned around and saw Derek's smiling face.

"Well, hello there," I said. Cenny was right behind him. "I see you're on the night shift. Hey, I would like you to meet someone." I turned to Andrea. "I met these two fellows earlier this afternoon, and they're funny little devils. The tall one is Derek, and that's Cenny!"

They reached out for her hand at the same time and fought a little about who would kiss it first. She found it very sweet and funny. "What would you like to drink, my lady?" Cenny asked her, kissing her hand another time.

"A pina colada would be fine," she answered with a smile.

"And what about you, Louise?"

"I'll take a mai tai," I said before turning toward Alain.

"Those two are quiet a pair, aren't they?" Alain said. By the look on his face, I wasn't sure what he said was true.

I replied, "Eh, yes, quite a pair." He looked away. I thought a change of subject would do him good. "So, Alain, what will we be eating tonight?"

"We're eating at the beach bar tonight. They're serving French food there. Would Andrea care to join us?"

"No, no, that's okay. I'll be just fine. Go on along and enjoy yourselves. I will eat up here with David and Andrew," Andrea answered.

"Oh, Alain, would you mind a lot if we took a look at the buffet up here? I heard it was a fish buffet, and I am dying to see how it has all been mounted. Vladimir, a German man I met yesterday, told me it was quite a sight and not to miss it. He's an old-timer vacationer in the club and was always amazed by the arrangements in this buffet." I gave him my pleasing look, which never failed to get me what I wanted. Andrea and I had long figured out being blonde here was just not enough, The ladies here were so gorgeous, and some were untouchable. They made us blondes look bad. But it was what it was.

"Of course we can go. Come on. I'll try to sneak us in before the big crowd reaches. It will give you a chance to see it all." Alain started leading the way.

"Have a nice dinner, and see you later," I told Andrea in one breath as I ran to catch up with Alain.

When I saw the buffet, I couldn't believe my eyes. How in the hell could they make such things with a single fish? On the first table, there was this gigantic sailfish mounted in a way that it seemed like it was jumping from the table. It was spectacular. All the tables had a specialty. One was decorated with various seafood, another held grouper, and there was even a tuna fish arrangement. The whole place looked like a fish market, with fish nets hinging everywhere and different kinds of

Yoann Pesant

plastic or dried fishes hanging here and there from the ceiling or in the net. I had to give credit to Vladimir. It sure was quite a sight.

In no time the restaurant was invaded by all the GGs. It was mere minutes before the crowd burst into the restaurant. There was no way we could leave by the entrance, so Alain led me to the back stairs. That was when Alain started holding my hand. At that point, I didn't know what to do or say, so I let it be. "Are you planning on diving tomorrow morning?" he asked me when we were walking on the path leading to the beach bar.

"Well, maybe I will in the afternoon. There's so much to do around here," I replied.

"Yeah, I know." We walked in silence for a while, and then he went on. "Your girlfriend and you seem to be hitting it pretty good. Have you known each other very long?"

"Since school. We're like sisters," I told him while we walked across the volleyball court and made our way to the entrance of the restaurant.

The chief of restaurant welcomed us warmly and found us a table for two complete with candlelight and wine. The lights were dimmed and helped creating a romantic atmosphere typical of French mentality. Before leaving, our host showed us where to get beer, Coca-Cola, or 7 Up. He left, but not before giving a knowing smile to Alain.

"Well, what would you like to drink?" Alain asked me.

"A little wine will be just great."

"So tell me a little about yourself," he went on as the waiter placed a soup in front of us.

"It depends what you would like to know."

"Why don't you tell me what you do back home?"

After taking a deep breath, I said, "At this time, not much. I lost my job right before leaving. A stupid argument over vacation days."

"That's too bad. Now what will you do?"

"Well, my father started a clothing business of his own. I guess I will join him for a while, to see if I like it."

The waiter brought us our main course, which consisted of filet mignon along with crevettes papillons in a wine and garlic sauce.

They were served on a bed of buttered rice, spiced to delight, and accompanied by baby carrots. It was a dream to the palate.

"And what about you? How long have you been in the club?" I asked between mouthfuls.

"Three years as a scuba instructor."

Eager to know more, I went on. "And will you be staying long in this village?"

"Usually it isn't more than a six-month stay."

"Oh? And why is that?"

He said, "Really, it's a policy in the club. A GS stays in one village. As a matter of fact, a whole team of GSs stays only for a period of six months in the same village. Staying longer would probably be too boring, and a change of village brings new horizons, which stimulates the mind."

"Even the chief of village?"

"Him too. He's also a GS but is in charge of the village. He has much more responsibility on his shoulders. He's the one making the final decisions."

We were silent for a while, enjoying our delicious meal while it was still hot. Then Alain came out with it. "I guess by now you know I like you a lot."

Not surprised, I said with a sweet smile, "Let's say I felt you didn't hate me."

"Do you think I'll be able to see you later?"

Not wanting to break the mood, I replied, "I will be around. But I want to tell you right away that what you want, I don't think I could give it to you." I thought to myself, *Boy, these guys do move fast around here.*

"Can I ask you a question?"

"Fire away."

He said, "Tell me what you think of me right now?"

"Right now, I think you're a nice person, and I do like you. But I don't really know you, just as you don't really know me. It takes time for people to get to know one another. I guess am old-fashioned, but I'm sincere to that. Does that make any sense to you?"

Yoann Pesant

"Very much, but how much time do you have left on your vacation?"

"About five more days."

"And do you think you would be able to get to know me in five days?"

Boy, is he sharp, I said to myself. "I don't know, Alain. It's just that the life here is so different than back home. You live in a paradise without problems. Back home, it's a rat race. That's why I came here: to get away from it all."

"You know, you are a very beautiful girl. I would like to get to know you better, and I'll take whatever time it requires."

"Alain, is it because I'm blonde?"

While looking at me, he said, "In these parts, blondes can be rear, but blonde hair still doesn't stand a chance. Look around you."

I knew he had a valid point. Still, I had to make it clear. "Alain, I have a boyfriend back home, and I don't know whether I would be able to live with myself if I did something I believe is wrong."

"Are you saying you wouldn't be able to live with yourself because of him?"

I looked Alain in the eyes and said, "It's the thought of knowing I was not honest with him."

"It's very good to think that way, but what goes on here stays here. It has nothing to do with your life back home." His way of thinking challenged my own.

"That's very difficult for me to believe in."

"Can you at least think it over for a while?" he said as he finished his meal.

"I will," I told him, and I busied myself with finishing my plate.

Dessert was served on a little plate which consisted of an assortment of French pastries—my favorite. We finished our meal by sipping espressos and exchanging jokes.

The night air felt good. *Cool as mint,* I thought. It was funny how my mind compared mint to the air around me. It had never occurred to me before, but the whole place was such a fantasy, it was no wonder my mind came out with a new vision of things.

We walked on the little path leading back to the main building, both content from the food. Alain took my hand again and made a stop. I looked at him and had a feeling he wanted to kiss me, but still I wasn't sure that's what I wanted.

"Thanks for dinner," he said. He quickly kissed me on the lips one time, then two times. then I bowed my head down before the third one came. "Is something wrong?" he said, placing his other hand under my chin to lift my head up slowly.

I had to say it. "It's just that I feel I'm not doing the right thing," I replied before biting a fingernail.

"Is there something wrong with kissing a person you like very much?" he argued.

"No."

"Then why won't you kiss me?" he asked, ready to try again.

"Please, Alain, not now. I would rather not talk about it for now." We started walking again.

We reached the main bar just as the music from the dance floor stopped, announcing it was soon show-time. I looked around for Andrea, but she was nowhere in sight. We decided to watch the show, so we followed the crowd and went to where Alain said was the most comfortable place in the theater, the back row, leaning on the back wall.

It was a lip-synching contest tonight. The lights went down, and the people were silent. The curtain lifted on the chief of village introducing the show and giving a quick rundown on the events to follow: a joke contest on the dance floor at eleven thirty, and then Mexican day tomorrow. Then it was on with the show. It was amazing to see all those GSs so full of talent and life. Participation from the audience was tremendous, and cheers brought up points for this number or that one. For Cenny and Dereck, their "Figaro" number won more cheers than all the others, which made them the big winners. They got out of cleaning dishes. That made me smile in memory of my afternoon encounter with them.

The show closed with those crazy signs. I was getting better at them because they took time to show it to us before going on like a fast-moving movie. They were giving prizes, such as a free week in the village to any GG who could come on stage and do those crazy signs without flaw, first each sign twice and then each sign once. It was very hard to do, but I was sure working on it to give it a try.

Music started on the dance floor, inviting everyone for a good dance. Alain and I did just that for a while before he excused himself to attend a scuba meeting. He made sure to tell me he would be back here, or else he'd be at the disco. I continued dancing, and in no time other GSs closed in on me. That was when I decided to leave the floor and go to the main bar.

As I waited for my pina colada, Andrea nudged me in my side, startling me. "Hey, you! So how are you doing, my dear?" I said, laughing.

"Not too bad, not too bad. I'm so full of fish, you wouldn't believe. The dinner was so good. Guess whom I dined with tonight?"

"Well? Aren't you gonna tell me?"

"Yoann, the GS working at the beach bar. You know—the big, tall, dark one."

"Oh, yes, I know whom you mean. I met him this morning."

"He sure has some interesting ways to look at life. I think he's a very special person, don't you think?"

"From what I saw, he sure looks different." Boy, I was so thirsty that I'd already finished my pina colada. No wonder my head was spinning. "How about dancing?"

"Good idea," Andrea told me, "but let me finish my drink first." In no time, she downed her drink, and we were almost flying to the dance floor. Unfortunately, as soon as we hit the dance floor, the music stopped. It was already eleven thirty—time for the joke contest. We laughed at our timing and decided to stay for a few jokes.

An hour and a thousand laughs later, we gaily headed to the discotheque, ready for some dancing. The place was so crowded that the dancing was simply moving our feet to the music. Still, I managed a few gracious body movements. Someone knocked on my shoulders, and I turned around and met Alain's charming eyes. "Well, hello there!" I yelled over the music. I had a habit of saying that.

"Hello, my beautiful one," he said near my ear.

When Andrea saw us together, she left the dance floor for the bar.

Alain and I danced for a while before doing the same thing as Andrea, and we headed for the bar to chat over drinks. It was around two when Alain offered me a walk on the beach, but I did not accept his offer, so as not to lead him on. I did accept his offer to sit outside by the pool, but only for a short while. I grabbed Andrea to let her in on my whereabouts and tell her I would meet her in the room in a short while.

The minute we approached the pool area, Alain looked at me and came out with it. "I get this feeling I will not share the night with you," he told me in disappointment.

"You are right about that," I replied as we continued walking.

"We don't have to make love tonight. We could just get to know each other better. Don't you trust me?"

"Well, yes. I do. As much as I know you, I do."

"Then what's the matter?"

"I don't trust myself. I hate starting something I cannot finish. Plus, I'm afraid of getting hurt."

We spoke a while longer, and then he asked if he could walk me to my room—but not before having tried very hard to bring me to his own room. When we reached my door, he told me, "I'm falling in love with you, Louise." I didn't know whether to believe him, but before he could continue, I quickly kissed him and then rushed into my room, closing the door behind me.

Fourteen

The exchange of trivial feelings

*A*ndrea arrived about fifteen minutes later. She found me already in bed and staring at the ceiling. "Well, well. What's all this wondering about?"

"He told me he's falling in love with me, but by living in a paradise like this, I wonder whether he says the same thing to every girl he meets. Have you noticed being blonde doesn't make a difference here?"

"Does he have a girlfriend?" Andrea asked, avoiding my question.

"I never asked him, but if he did, why would he be spending time with me?" "Maybe he likes blondes." She grinned at me before continuing. "I'll take that one back because the European girls here are so beautiful, even blondes don't stand a chance. Maybe it's something else."

"So how about David?" I asked her.

"He's a fool, but I like him. I don't know. I guess time will answer that for me,"

I wanted to laugh when she said he was a fool because I understood so well. "It's always the fool one who gets you," I said. "I saw Andrew on my way here. He just woke up and said that David was still in bed, snoring. They both missed dinner, so he was going down by the disco for those late-night hamburgers."

"You know, I like David, but he doesn't seem to like being sober. They both drink beer all day long," she said, a bit disappointed.

I said to myself, *Drinking beer all day, he must be a fool.* I had always backed away from that quotation because it hurt me, and just maybe that quotation meant much more to me than I wanted to believe. Still, I went on to say, "And how about Paul? Did you see him?"

"He was at the disco with that girl. Remember her? Anyway, he seems to be a wild guy taking advantage of every girl he meets. I'm just about to give up the ghost about him!" She made her way into the bathroom and shouted, "He looks like a dead-end by my book!"

"By my book too," I replied, and we both burst out laughing.

When she came out of the bathroom ready for bed, I said, "What would you say if we played a little tennis tomorrow morning?"

"Sounds good to me. Ten o'clock would be fine, don't you think? And we should be down for breakfast at nine to feel in shape around ten."

"Great," I answered. "Oh, and listen, girl! You got away with paying for the drinks tonight! You remember our bet, don't you?"

After pausing for one breath, she said, "Well, you know how things turn out sometimes!"

"Yeah, sure!" We started laughing.

"Don't worry," she went on. "I'll meet the bet—tonight, if you want."

"Well, girlfriend, we should get some sleep, don't you think? Or else we won't wake up for tomorrow's program."

She said, "You're right. Have sweet dreams."

"Same to you." I turned over in bed and fell asleep like a rock.

Yoann Pesant

Fifteen

The tennis players

The next morning, we were all set to leave for breakfast at nine sharp. When we were seated by the hostess, we were not surprised to find ourselves sitting with none other than David and Andrew. That was to Andrea's great pleasure.

"You girls look like champagne and champions this morning," David said, noticing our tennis outfit.

"Well I'm surprised you're up so early and look so well," Andrea said while nibbling on a piece of cheese.

"That's because I slept all the sourness out of my body, my dear! I feel like a new man right now, ready to push mountains!"

"You don't have to go to that extent, you know," Andrea told him, laughing.

"What would you say, if we took on you both in a tennis match?" Andrew asked us. It made us both look at him and smile.

"Yeah, how about it, girls?" David agreed, quite confident in himself.

"You really think you two could take us on?" Andrea challenged.

"We can take you on in more than just tennis," David answered with one of those kinky looks.

"Losers pay champagne—the best," Andrea answered him, holding his gaze bravely.

"That's a deal," David told her, not backing down. We all shook hand on it. "We'll meet you at the tennis courts around ten. We both have to change." They finished up their breakfast and left the table.

We quickly finished our breakfast to head out on the tennis courts and get in a quick warm-up before our playmates reached us. We took on the bet without even knowing what kind of players they were. We were not too bad ourselves, but at least we looked the part, dressed like true professional tennis players.

At ten sharp, both of them were ready for action.

The game lasted only half an hour because the heat was so intense and made it very hard to play a violent game like tennis. We each had only one more point to win the game, but they scored first. We had a lot of fun playing, and of course we had to pay for the champagne. We headed merrily to the bar, and the guys carried on about the way they'd won the game. We laughed at the way they carried on like children. Andrea looked a little upset, and in my ear she reminded me, "He's a fool."

To compensate for her feelings, I whispered back, "But he's your fool." We laughed at each other. It was the first time I'd ever drunk champagne in the morning, and I loved it. Andrea was getting a little giddy over it, and I was well on my way too.

By eleven, the bottle was finished, and Andrea and I were ready to set sail to the arts and crafts shop before it closed. We hurried to our room to change into something more comfortable. We left the room, and Andrea decided to stop at the excursion office to book the horseback riding trip, which was scheduled at five o'clock every afternoon. While Andrea signed up for her trip, I asked more about the excursions. The girl talked for the next fifteen minutes about all the excursions available: the deep-sea fishing trip for a half or a full day, and the sunset cruise on the Pacific with champagne and romantic music. But when it came down to the outside excursions to Guadalajara, Puerto Vallarta, or Barra de Navidad, I stopped her right there. Time was not on my side for this, and Andrea was waiting for me. I thanked her nicely, and we were on our way. Andrea went to the silk painting shop, and I headed to the boutique. It would do me good to spend a little bit on goodies for my family and friends—and maybe a piece or two for me, of course.

Sixteen

Meeting Yoann again

I went back to the room to dump my goodies, put on my bathing suit, and try on my new pareu. I wanted to laze around on the beach before the big Mexican lunch party.

The sand felt very hot under my naked feet, and I ran to soothe them where the water soaked the sand. There were a few sailboats out, and a lesson was going on near the sailing shack. It was so peaceful around here. I could never get enough of this peace and the beauty that surrounded me. I could walk for hours on seashore, lost in nature's fascinating attraction. It was all so fragile, yet it had been around for centuries. For example, birds didn't have to work like us, yet they were always taken care of and were never at a loss for food. I found that more than fascinating.

When I neared the beach bar, I decided to treat me to a cool pina colada. It's a good thing I thought to bring my bar beads. I entered the bar and spotted Yoann sitting in the far corner. I went for my drink and then headed straight to where he was sitting.

"Hello, stranger," he said with that bright smile as I approached his table.

"How is it you are not working?" I asked him, smiling back.

"A gentle staff is always on duty, you know. Now, tell me, how was your morning?"

"Well, my girlfriend Andrea and I played tennis this morning with some friends and lost. She's at the silk painting now. She told me you had dinner last night together, and she found you very interesting."

He shifted in his seat. "I don't think I was that interesting, but I thought she was a very interesting person," he replied, and we both laughed.

"I can see you two understand each other."

"Tell me, how is your boyfriend doing?"

That came as a surprise, however I smiled and replied, "If you mean here in Playa, I don't have one."

"How about Alain? Did you enjoy your dinner last night?"

His words made me wonder for a minute. "How did you know about that? You were not here yesterday night," I quickly replied.

"How do you know I wasn't in here yesterday night for dinner?" he gently answered.

"Because I looked around, and you were nowhere in sight." *Got out of that one*, I thought while awaiting his answer.

"Well, I passed through for a short while and spotted you with him. When I looked at you, I couldn't blame the guy for wanting more than dinner with you. You see, it was written all over his face."

"Why do you say that? Is it the only thing men around here think about?"

"I can't answer that because each man has his own mind and desires."

"You have a point, but I don't wish to comment on it. Why don't you come and sit or walk under the sun with me?"

That did not come out totally right, I thought.

Yoann replied, "I'll sit in the shade with you. As you can see, I don't need a tan." We got up and made our way to the nearest tree near the ocean.

"So how long have you been a GS?" I asked him, stretching in my lounging chair.

"It's been five years."

"So that means you've been to about ten clubs already. Do you know how many clubs there are around the world?" I asked him.

"The club has villages in twenty-five countries around the world. In all, there should be about 102 villages, with many more to come in the near future.

"Wow. Talk about a big company! And do you know who owns Club Vacation?"

"Today, 35 percent of the clubs are owned by main shareholders, both French and foreign. The others are held by various stockholders, including many club members."

"Do you know who started with the idea of the Club Vacation?"

"A man named Gerard Gray."

"And he started it all alone?"

"Well, Gerard Gray started it in 1950, and then he was joined by Gill Trigo in 1954. That is the history. Those two men made Club Vacation what it is today."

More curious, I said, "Have you ever met any of them?"

"I've met Gill Trigo a few times. He's a very nice man and used to pass through many villages to give meetings to GSs about the club."

"Well, I can say you do have a very nice life here. This place is so beautiful. Every GS seems to be happy and smiling. How does the club choose good GSs? In other words, what is a good GS?"

"Let's just say it could be done if you make it possible," he replied.

"You do have a good way of thinking," I told him. I noticed on my watch that it was almost noon. "Would you care to join us for lunch at the garden party?" I asked him, wishing he would agree.

"It would be a pleasure, my dear. But if you want to see the beginning of it, we'd better go right now." We both got up, I fixed my pareu in a nice fashion, and we headed to the garden party.

The opening of the Mexican garden party was magnificent. There was a parade around the garden by the mariachis, which were the country's folkloric singers and dancers. They started to parade on horses, and then they unsaddled to form a dance formation. They were dancing and whirling away. It was beautiful. The dresses of the girls were so flamboyant with colors, and the men's costumes were exactly what I had always imagined, with those big sombreros and little vests embroidered in a Mexican fashion. I turned my smiling face toward Yoann to share my wonder at it all. He seemed to find more pleasure in my amazement than in the show itself, because when I turned he was already looking intently at me with a curious smile on his face. It made me shy for a second or two, but my attention was brought back to the dancing.

I almost forget about Andrea until I saw her searching face in the distance. I waved in her direction to attract her attention because yelling would be to no avail with all this music going on. After a while, she finally noticed me and came toward us. She was surprised to see Yoann, but it was written all over her face how happy she was to see him again. Knowing Andrea as I did, I could see she liked Yoann more than she cared to tell me. That troubled me, but I didn't quite understand why.

As soon as the show was finished, the chief of the village made the announcement that the buffet was opened. All the GGs then started admiring the variety of food set on tables surrounding the garden, leaving the middle free, where they had set blankets for everyone to sit on just like a real picnic. It did not take long for everyone to start packing food on their plates because everything looked so appetizing. We started touring the tables, wondering where to start. There were dozens of tables holding mounds of food that begged to be tasted. And the dessert tables were more than incredible. Andrea and I looked at each other and had the same thought: *To hell with gaining pounds.* We wanted to taste as much of everything as possible.

The lunch was the most filling we'd had yet, and the most cheerful. The three of us got to know each other very well while sitting, laughing, and eating. I started to look at Yoann with new eyes. I wondered whether I was falling in love with him, but that could not be because it would undermine everything I had told Alain and myself. Like David to Andrea, I would be a fool. That was the disturbing thought I was so afraid of. I had to take hold of myself. I found him to be a very resourceful man, and I liked that. He was also calm and sure of himself, but not in an awkward way. I felt good near him. It would be my secret for the time being.

After this nice lunch, Yoann excused himself. Andrea and I left to see the pareu demonstration. I didn't see anyone else wearing a pareu like Yoann did. We needed to learn all those funny ways to wear them. After the end of the demonstration, we were accosted by David and

Andrew, who absolutely wanted us as partners for the sand sculpture contest. We headed for the beach and entered the contest. A half hour later, we were the winners of a bottle of champagne for the best sand sculpture, a gigantic crocodile. I suggested keeping the bottle in my room for a good occasion because we knew those two guys could not be counted on when it came to alcohol. We all agreed. David wanted to take Andrea sailing, and Andrew was going for a tennis match, so I offered to take the bottle to the room.

The cool of the air-conditioned room felt good after the heat of the day. I lay on my bed for a while, letting my mind wonder with thoughts of Yoann and Alain, and in no time I fell asleep. It wasn't until I heard the bathroom door closing that I opened my eyes again to Andrea getting herself ready for horseback riding. It was now twenty to five.

"How was the sailing?" I asked her as she opened the door again.

"Oh, girl, it was great! Tomorrow I'm taking courses. You should try it. I'm sure you would like it. Did you sleep well?"

"Yeah. I guess I was more tired than I cared to admit because it took two minutes, and I was out like a light."

"What do you say we both take a course of sailing tomorrow morning, Louise?"

"Well, it did look kind of fun when I saw people sailing this morning. Yeah, okay, it's a deal for tomorrow morning. Do you believe it will be the first thing we do together?"

"You're right; I didn't even notice it before. But it won't really be together because we each have a sailing boat. Make sure you follow me."

"I'll make sure to stay afloat. I'm sure I will have plenty in my hand just doing it." We both agreed and laughed.

"Well, I'm leaving for the horseback riding. What will you be doing?" Andrea asked me.

"I want to join the volleyball games, and then I'll meet you back here around six thirty."

"By the way, Alain was asking for you. He said something about scuba diving tomorrow," she said while at the door's threshold.

"Where did you meet him?" I asked.

"On my way up here. Take care. I'll see you later," she said, and then she left the room.

I got myself ready and left for the volleyball court. The game was already started, to my disappointment. I took a seat on the grass and enjoyed the scene anyway. In no time, Alain showed up beside me. I was a bit surprised to see him but guessed he'd spotted me from afar. "Hello there, beautiful. I have to say you are a very hard girl for me to find," he said a bit seriously.

I had to come up with something. "I wasn't very far. I was around here all day. How was the scuba this afternoon?"

"I waited for you," he replied.

"I'm sorry. I fell asleep up in my room," I told him.

"I'm going up to my room for a quick shower. Will you be here when I return?" he said, looking me over.

I told him, "If I'm not here, I'll be up at the solarium for some classical music."

He quickly gave me a kiss on my cheek before leaving.

SEVENTEEN

The request, the Solarium, the romance

*W*hen the game finished, I went to the beach bar to order a drink. I didn't want to admit to myself it was Yoann I wanted to see. I headed to the bar, and there he was, this time behind the bar. The minute our eyes met, we lit up with smiles.

"You are exactly the person I wanted to see," he told me with that charming smile of his. "I have something to ask you."

I interjected. "First, I would like a pina colada, please." I gave my most charming smile.

"Coming up!" he said.

"So, what is it you want to ask me, Yoann?" I asked as he handed me my glass.

After he cleared his throat jokingly, he said, "Would you like to have dinner with me at the Zapatha tonight?"

"I would be more than honored to accompany you," I said, making it sound light and cheerful even though my heart skipped a few beats and my mouth suddenly felt very dry. I gulped down my drink faster than I should have, and my head started to spin a little. "What will we be having for dinner at this restaurant?" I inquired, smiling.

"Their specialty is Mexican food."

"Isn't it Mexican food at the main restaurant tonight?"

"Yes, but at the main restaurant, it's tables for eight. At the Zapatha, it's tables for two," he replied, smiling.

I smiled back at him and took the last sip from my glass. "Say, Yoann, can you tell me where I can find the solarium?"

"I will show you where it is," he said, and then he called out for someone to replace him until his return.

We had to pass in front of the snorkeling shack to gain access to the stairway leading to the solarium. On the stairway, Yoann asked me to close my eyes, which I did, and he led me to the top. Then I felt his lips on mine ever so softly. It took me by surprise, and my eyes popped open. That was when I saw the view, and it was breathtaking. I could see over the whole village, surrounded by the beauty of the landscape and the sea. The sight was out of this world. The classical music added a touch of reality to it all.

"It's true what they say: the Club Vacation is a great vacation environment unlike any other, a wonderful escape from the busy world, and the perfect climate for body and soul peace," he said as he also admired the scenery.

"Is that what the club is for you?" I asked him, looking at him in the eyes.

"To me the club is the future because people will always be in need of a change of pace, and this place can offer it."

We sat for a while chatting, wanting these moments to last forever, but he had to get back to his work. We headed back to the beach bar. Just as Yoann went behind the bar, Alain walked into the place to meet me. "I was looking for you out there," he told me, showing me the volleyball court.

"I told you I went to look at the solarium," I replied, waving to Yoann as I walked with Alain toward the court.

"You know Yoann?" Alain asked me, trying to sound unconcerned.

"We met a few times. He's a very nice person," I told him while looking at the second game of volleyball, which was in its last round.

"So, Louise, how about dinner tonight?" Alain eagerly asked me.

"Thanks anyway, Alain, but Yoann invited me to eat with him tonight," I replied. I noticed by the expression on his face that he wasn't too pleased.

We talked for a little while, until they made up the teams for the last game of volleyball. By the time I finished playing the game, Alain was nowhere in sight. As I was leaving, Yoann approached me to set our rendezvous for eight o'clock at the Zapatha restaurant.

It was seven when I entered my room, and I hurried into the shower before Andrea arrived. I took care with my appearance because this was a special occasion. I wanted to be at my best for Yoann, though I didn't really understand why it was so important. Or maybe I didn't want to admit to myself the reason why I was doing and feeling all this. I pushed these thoughts out of my mind to greet Andrea as she walked in. It was already a little past seven thirty, and she didn't have much time to get herself ready for dinner. I told her I was having dinner with Yoann at the Zapatha before she got in the shower. Because I was all set, I shouted to her I would see her later in the evening. I knew she was in good hands with David. What I didn't know was whether the fool was David or me. Blocking it all out, I left the room blonde, bold, and beautiful to have a little bit of time on my own before meeting Yoann.

The main bar was crowded with people. I had about twenty minutes in front of me before my dinner. I heard a voice calling my name, and when I looked, it was Cenny sitting on top of that same bench again, but this time he was alone. "Well, hello there, Cenny. I haven't seen you for a while," I told him with a smile as I walked toward him.

"Were you looking for me?" he teased.

"How about you? Were you looking for me?" I replied.

He shouted, "Yes, I was looking for you from the day you came here, just to let you know how much I love you! But of course, you don't have time for me. What do you want me to do? Wait for you?" Then he calmly went on. "If so, just tell me. Whenever you're ready for me, I'll be here!" While he was talking, he held my hand and played with it in a desperate fashion. It was only when he burst out laughing that I realized he was joking. I playfully smacked him for his bad behavior.

At that moment, a girl approached him and kissed his lips. *It must be his girlfriend,* I thought given the way he looked at her, so soft and tender. She then looked at me and said hello. By her accent, I knew she was French.

"Darling, I would like you to meet Louise. She was just asking me for information about the village," Cenny told her, lying his head off, out of the situation. She stood staring at me.

"I'd better be going. You two enjoy the night, and thanks again for the information," I said, looking at Cenny before walking away. I had to bail him out. From the bar, I noticed he had a lot of explaining to do in order to make her believe him.

When I looked at my watch, it was eight o'clock. Yoann was already waiting for me when I walked to the entrance of the restaurant, which was not far from the main bar. We were seated in a far corner of the restaurant on a table for two, surrounded by natural vegetation and flowers. It was a buffet, so we got up to get ourselves plates full of exquisite Mexican specialties, which were very tasty but also very spicy. While we ate, a group of mariachis came along and played lovely Mexican tunes while some escorting GSs passed from table to table, along with the chief of sports, to fill shot glasses with tequila. Everybody toasted in union while the chief of sports played drunk, and the group of GSs joked around with the GGs. It was so funny.

"Boy, all I see around here are more new faces among the GS. How many are you together?" I asked him, amazed.

"Oh, we're about one hundred GSs from all over the world, and maybe two hundred local people," he answered.

"By the way, all you GS seem to be so happy. I guess once you work your first season, you don't want to quit, hey? I mean, this is so great, so beautiful. City life must not be appealing anymore," I noted.

"I'll be honest with you: it really depends on the individual. Not everyone is cut for this type of work, and not everybody wants it for a long period of time. Take me, for example. I have been with the club for over five years, and right now my goal is to be chief of village one day." He seemed very confident.

"I'm sure you will be a very good one indeed," I assured him.

"Well, thank you, my dear," he said softly while looking into my eyes.

We had a very pleasant dinner that was not one full of undercurrent; it was honest and simple. We felt like we'd known each other for years, even though I had a lot to learn from him, and him from me. But every good thing had an end. We walked to the bar for espressos and danced to soft music on the nine thirty dance floor of the small amphitheater.

During the show, we sat very close together. I found it hard to concentrate on the wonderful spectacle the mariachis were performing, which was a very colorful and pleasant show. Mexicans knew how to enjoy themselves.

Yoann left me to join the GSs in doing the crazy signs at the end of the show, but we met again on the dance floor for a few dances. I spotted Andrea dancing with David at the other end of the floor. She didn't even notice me, but I could see she was having a good time. Yoann and I were enjoying ourselves like little children, dancing, laughing, and showing off our talents as if we wanted to impress the other in the worst way.

We left the dance floor out of breath, and Yoann offered me a drink. We went to the crowed bar, and as Yoann was ordering the drinks, Alain approached me, taking the liberty to hold my hand. My heartbeat acted up. I didn't like the situation I was in right now. "Will you be at the disco for the Brazilian night?" he asked me, placing his other hand on my waist.

"What is the Brazilian night?" I asked him, kindly moving on the opposite side of Yoann to avoid Alain's sneaky hand.

"It's a big limbo contest, and it's a lot of fun," he replied while Yoann turned around and handed me my drink.

"Alain! How are things going?" Yoann said, standing between us without a clue.

"Good," Alain replied, looking at Yoann and then at me as if he was jealous.

"How about a drink?" Yoann asked him kindly.

"No, that's okay," he replied before walking away.

"What's wrong with him?" Yoann stated, looking at me.

I replied, "I think it has something to do with me. He wanted to have dinner with me tonight, but I declined because I was already busy with you."

Thinking nothing much of it, Yoann said, "That's life, I suppose.

Now, would you like to see the Brazilian night at the disco, or walk around a little?" He had a slight smile on his face.

"Walking around a little sound good to me," I said to ease tension, "especially after all that dancing."

As we left the bar, I glimpsed Cenny at his usual place on those benches, stopping every girl passing his way. When Yoann and I passed, he looked at Yoann and pointed his finger at me while saying, "Bad luck, bad luck!" It made me laugh.

"What is Cenny talking about now?" Yoann asked while walking out to the swimming pool.

"I think he had trouble with his girlfriend tonight. She caught him talking and laughing with me, and I guess she did not believe we were doing nothing wrong," I said as we passed the swimming pool and headed to the beach.

"Flirting would be more appropriate for Cenny. As for his girlfriend, she is a very jealous person. That's why she acts like that, but she too will be okay," Yoann said in a mannerly way.

"I think he's a very funny person. Every time I see him, I laugh so much, and those dark eyebrow of his kill me."

"I always tell him he should be more on stage," Yoann said, holding my hand as we walked on the sandy beach.

Eighteen

Under the stars

T he romance of the stars glittering across the white sand gave light to a romantic beach, and the moonlight settled in for the night. "It's so beautiful out here, Yoann," I reiterated while looking around at all this beauty in one place like a canvas ready for its painter.

After looking around and at me, he whispered, "It's like this almost every night, you know." He took hold of my right hand and kissed it before uttering, "You are so beautiful. You should see how the moonlight sparkles against your blonde hair."

I gently caressed my puffed blonde hair. He could not have said it at a better time. My hand gently moved down my face, with one finger silently gliding across my lower lip, I almost pleaded, "Please don't say anything more." My eyes got glossy because I knew I was in trouble. His words touched me like lightning, and it showed in my expression. "You called me by my name." That meant so much to me, and my head and heart bowed down to him.

At that, he stopped me, placed himself in front of me, lifted my head, looked in my eyes, and kissed me. I saw it coming, but I was hopeless. His lips were so soft and sweet that I couldn't resist them. Yes, kissing him made me want him more, but the thought of my boyfriend brought me back to reality. For a quick minute, my mind flashed back to what Andrea had called David, a fool. *But I like Yoann. Am I a fool for doing so, or am I being fooled? I need help, and it's only me and Yoann standing here.* I whispered, "Please, Yoann, stop me, help me. I have a boyfriend back home."

He then placed his arms around me and whispered tenderly in my ear, "We are here now." Then he kissed me again. At this moment, there was nothing I wanted more than to be kissed and loved in his tight embrace.

The next two hours were ecstatic, with the moon, the stars, and the ocean breeze for companions. At one point, we found ourselves in the water for a night swim. I felt like I was in a dream from which I didn't want to wake up. We talked so much, and it was so interesting. And his kisses were so passionate. Now I knew I was falling in love—and I was in even more trouble.

We decided to make a short visit to the night club for a few dances before turning in for the night. Even at three in the morning, the place was going wild. I looked around to see if I could spot Andrea, but to no avail. I guessed at this time she was fast asleep in bed.

After such a calm and peaceful time on the beach, the disco was too wild for our mood. Yoann offered to accompany me back to my room. I jumped at the chance of being with him a little longer, and I thanked my maker I didn't run into Alain along the way.

On my doorstep, we talked for a while and then hugged and kissed goodnight. I entered my room. Andrea was already fast asleep, so I tiptoed my way to bed, rocked by thoughts of Yoann. I remembered closing my eyes and opening them again at the thoughts of my words to Alain. *But I want to tell you right away that what you want, I don't think I could give to you. It takes time for people to get to know each other.* Was I the fool here? *Somebody, anybody help me.* I soon passed out like a light.

NINETEEN

The Shaking, the awaking.

I was awoken the next morning because everything shook. Through my sleep, I realized it was Andrea shaking me to wake up. "Louise, wake up!" she said. "We have an appointment together, remember? We are supposed to go sailing this morning. We should be there at nine, so hurry up. We need to grab a fast breakfast."

"What time is it?"

"It's eight thirty. Time to wake up!"

"My God. Do you know what time I went to bed? It was past three thirty. I completely forgot about the sailing this morning. Oh, Andrea, I had a wonderful night last night!"

"Yes, well, how about telling me about it on our way out of here?"

It was hard, but I regained enough energy to shake off the sleep, and in no time we were seated in the restaurant for a light breakfast. Then we headed to the sailing shack. Andrea told me she wanted to finish her silk pareu after the sailing course. "Yeah, that's a good idea. I will go too. I almost forgot about mine."

Paul was more than pleased when he saw us coming. "At last, you two finally decided to try the best sport there is!"

"The best sport after horseback riding," Andrea told him teasingly.

That brought a smile to his face. "You will see, my dear. After this course, you will change your mind."

"That's what you think," she went on. "Have you ever been riding around here to say that? You see, I'm a nature lover, and throughout the ride, all I saw was beauty beyond beauty. Flowers blossoming everywhere, and palm trees ripe with coconuts. We even passed through a small Mexican village and then a beautiful little forest. To finish off the magnificent ride, we came to this charming beach. I have never seen such a gorgeous place in my life. The sea as far as the eye can see, caressing a beach as white as sand can be, stretching as if it would never end. We raced our horses on the edge of the water, splashing cool spray at each other. It was like a movie, I tell you, and I loved every minute of it."

"Okay, okay. Easy, there. I believe you—don't say any more." He laughed, seeing how involved in her belief she seemed to be. "You two let me know when you are ready for this course, okay!"

I motioned to a nearby chair, but Andrea stopped me before I made a second step. "Louise, hold on. We'll start now, if that's okay with you, Paul."

"Whenever you want. I promise you nature lovers that you will not regret your choice. You will see many beautiful sights, but let's just say you will be seeing them at a different angle: from the sea instead of the land."

Paul went on with his course. He started by giving us the basics of sailing right here on the beach. He then showed us a sailboat, all its parts, and how to operate each piece. By the end of a half hour, we knew enough about sailing to try our luck on our own. We were each given a sailboat big enough for one, and Paul stayed on the shore, giving us instructions. Mistakes were made, but we soon felt confident enough to venture a little farther than the shoreline. It was quite a thrill, I must admit, and it was true what Paul said about the sights to admire, though I had other things to think about at this time—like making sure I didn't tip over. The water was so clear it was possible to catch glimpses of schools of fish of all sorts of colors and shapes. One thing I liked about this place was I didn't see one jellyfish during my vacation. Andrea seemed to be very intent on her sailing abilities. At one point, we almost had one heck of a collision. After an hour of this turning in circles, we opted to go back to the security of the land. It was already ten thirty, and we both wanted to finish the pareus we'd started at the arts and crafts shop.

We thanked Paul warmly for his great teaching abilities and most of all for his patience. I would never have imagined sailing on my own so quickly if it hadn't been for Paul.

We left the sailing shack in a rush to get to the silk painting as quickly as possible, in order to finish the coloring of our pareus before the closing hour. When I saw my design again, I was proud of it. It consisted of a parrot standing on a branch surrounded with green foliage. The background was a very clear red, and the parrot itself seemed alive with such warm colors. I put a final touch on the foliage. Andrea was a little more inventive and was more of an artist than I was. Hers looked more like a piece of art. It was a scene that seemed taken out of an Egyptian story, all in peaches and down-to-earth colors. It was beautiful. Everyone praised her work when she put down her brush. The things we could do with so little were amazing. As we cleaned our instruments, I told Andrea that I would meet her in the dining room. I was faster than her, so I rushed out of the shop toward the beach bar. I had but one thing in my mind: to meet Yoann and maybe even have lunch with him. Maybe I shouldn't have told Andrea I was to meet her, because I had no intention right now to share Yoann with her. Not that I was afraid of her, but I had so little time left in this village to be with him. I wanted all the time for myself, even if i was a fool. I didn't even tell her how involved I felt about him, and that was the action of a fool. I hoped she didn't think I didn't want her company. It was just that right now, I didn't wish to share my thoughts with anyone, not even with her. I'd make it up to her later on.

TWENTY

The search, the ping pong, my visitor

hen I reached the beach bar, it wasn't Yoann behind the bar. I was told that he'd already left. I was so disappointed and didn't know what to do. *Where could he be?* I thought. *Maybe in the dining room?* I made my way to the dining room. It was now twelve fifteen, and I was beginning to get hungry. When I reached the dining room, I looked everywhere for Yoann, but he was nowhere in sight. I spotted Andrea at a table that was already full. I let the hostess place me and my plate of goodies at a table where the chief of village was having his meal. It was quite an honor for me to be at his table. He was so charming and attentive to his guests. We all had a nice chat and a few laughs, and then he excused himself to attend to business.

I also made my way out and looked around in the restaurant, but Andrea had already left. I headed to the room for a quick change for the ping-pong tournament, and when I reached the room, Andrea wasn't there. The ping-pong tournament was scheduled for two o'clock, so I had an hour in front of me. I decided to take a stroll on the beach before the tournament.

The tournament lasted about an hour and a half. I did not win but had a great time. I was exhausted after that and a bit warm, so I headed to the beach and went directly in the water after leaving my sneakers and my pareu on a lounging chair. The water felt so good on my hot skin. I liked the way the ocean made body weight almost nonexistent. I floated for a while, enjoying this time of peacefulness to relax my body and mind. I went back to the lounging chair and lay out under the warm sun, letting the rays caress my body in a warm embrace.

I was taken away from my thoughts by a voice I knew well enough to make my heart miss a few beats. "Hello, stranger," he said to me, blocking the sun with his body. He had a way of coming at me in the most unexpected moments, but I was very pleased to see him.

"Well, hello there. How did you know I was here?"

"I could notice you lying among a thousand people."

I sat up, looking at him and wondering how in the hell he could be in such a good shape. "Tell me, Yoann, how do you keep yourself in this great shape? Do you lift weights or something?"

"Well, not really weights. It's through dancing and exercising with great big logs I find on the opposite side of the beach," he told me, showing me the left side of the beach.

"Logs?" I repeated. "What could be done with a log, of all things?"

"Yes, dear, logs."

"I see. Where are you going now?"

Yoann said, "I want to change to play basketball. But I really came here to ask you if I could see you later."

He didn't had to ask me twice. "Sure, I would like that."

"Would you like for us to have dinner together?"

"That would be good," I stammered while looking up at him.

He went on to say, "By the way, if you want to see Andrea, she was part of the treasure hunt at two thirty. It should be finished by now." So was one of my fingernails in my mouth. He kneeled down to give me a kiss before leaving, and I let it be.

I looked at him as he walked away, and then I realized I was in trouble with myself. I knew if I got emotionally involve, I would get hurt when the time came to say goodbye, but I was still fooling myself. People said that the danger zone was in the red, and so were my eyes. Yes, I wanted to cry because I was slowly losing this battle of control, and I was too afraid to tell even myself. *Help, help!* I wanted to shout, but I couldn't.

I lay again in the sun and was taken away from my thoughts by buzzing activity not far from my chair. As I looked, I saw a few GSs dressed as bumblebees, buzzing their way through the GGs carrying trays of fruits. I was more than pleased to be able to munch on pieces of mango and papaya while we were entertained by their buzzing act.

After a few swims and a good tanning session, I figured I would meet Andrea back at the room and ask her to accompany me on the sunset walk scheduled at five o'clock. When I reached the room, she wasn't in, so I put on a summer dress over my bathing suit, grabbed my purse, and made my way to the entrance of the village in time for the departure. I was surprised to see so many people for this walk. We were to walk to Careyes, which was about fifteen minutes away from the club. One GS led the group. The walk was surely worthwhile. It was a very exotic little village where it was possible to buy little souvenirs made by the local people. On the way back, we admired the beautiful sunset, splashing the skies with red and orange of all different shades, like the international day line crossing from day into night in a plane in the sky. It was quite a sight. We returned to the club around six. I didn't join the others at the bar because I wanted to take my time in preparing myself for my dinner date. I entered the room convinced I would meet Andrea, but she still wasn't in, and by the time I was ready to go at seven thirty, there was still no sign of her.

As I reached the bar, I was greeted by Cenny and his usual jokes. He offered me my drink and left to serve his other customers. "Don't work too hard!" I told him as he went to serve the guy in front of me. I took a few sips of my drink, looking around to see if I couldn't spot Yoann amid the crowd, but I didn't. I chatted a while with people I had met through my stay.

Someone tapped on my shoulders, and I turned to gaze into the beautiful eyes of my dearest Yoann. I smiled sweetly at him, and he greeted me with a kiss on my nose. Cenny shot me a funny look. We talked a while before making our way to the dining room, where a French buffet awaited us.

TWENTY-ONE

Dinner after ladies night

inner went by peacefully enough, but that little voice inside my head kept nagging at me about my boyfriend back home. I didn't listen. We were seated with a bunch of people coming directly from Dallas. Jokes were made about J.R. and his team from the TV show. Apart from that, they asked so many questions of Yoann regarding his life in the club that I hardly had time to speak to him. We left the table around a quarter to ten and barely made two dances on the dance floor before the show began. That night, the GSs put on an unbelievable cabaret filled with fun and laughter. I really enjoyed it. The whole amphitheater resounded with laughter and joyous cries.

When it was time for the crazy signs, Yoann was surprised to see I had them down pretty well. Only when it was time to make those signs once did I mess up.

The dance floor was crowded that night, so Yoann and I sat as spectators and chatted a while. I caught sight of Andrea dancing with Devon, the barman. David was not far away, and by the look on his face, he didn't seem to like seeing them together. Turning back to Yoann, I said, "So what's on the agenda for tonight?"

"You ladies have a special treat at the disco. Its ladies' night, with special entertainment. I'll leave it as a surprise. You will see. You should like it. There will also be fun games right here for the guys."

"Will you be part of that surprise at the disco?"

He smiled at me. "No, no. My mommy doesn't like me to do those kinds of things," he replied, acting his part so nicely that it made me laugh. He broke the act and laughed along with me.

I changed the subject. "Yoann, tell me something. I notice most of the GS speak two languages. Is it called for in their jobs?"

"Two languages are nothing. The people visiting the club come from all over the world, and they expect to be able to communicate with us. Some GSs speaks up to ten languages. Amazing, isn't it?"

"Where do you all find the time to learn them?"

"Well, usually there are teachers in many of the villages to teach the language of the country, but mostly it is among the people that words are captured and memorized, slowly but surely."

"Boy, it really is a terrific life you have here."

At that moment, the dance floor was stopped for the fun and games to begin. Yoann had to give a helping hand in setting up those games, so I headed down to the ladies' night special surprise. I tried to look for Andrea, but I guessed she'd already left the area.

I reached the crowded disco. Girls were everywhere, and as I stepped to the bar, what little light there was dimmed to nothing. On a prearranged stage, lights shot to reveal a male striptease. Girls started to shout their excitement at this good-looking surprise. I'd never seen this GS before, but I heard from the women around me that he worked in the repair shop. *So that's what Yoann was talking about*, I said to myself. I had to admit the guy was good. He knew every trick in the book, it seemed, and the audience responded to his every move. I spotted Andrea for a brief minute or two, but it was almost impossible to make a way through this crowd. The show lasted about an hour, where muscles were shown and G-strings were fortunately kept on. It was good entertainment and not an indecent number, but it gave the girls something to talk about.

"So how did you enjoy the little show?" Yoann asked. He was waiting for me at the entrance of the disco when it finished. He took my hand and led me on.

"It was very enjoyable. Is this show on every week?"

"Every two weeks. A lot of people come here for a two-week stay, so we try to make the entertainment program different for at least two weeks."

"Where are we going? Are we going for another late-night walk?"

He continued leading me on without a word, and my legs couldn't stop me. After a while, he said, "I have to make a stop at my place." I didn't say anything. In the back of my head, that little voice told me what was about to happen, but like so many other times, I didn't want to listen to it. On our way to his room, we made small talk.

"Did you see your girlfriend tonight?" he asked.

"I spotted her in the disco, but there were so many people in there, it was impossible to squeeze my way through. We haven't seen each other all day—since the silk painting, that is. It's like she's staying away from me. But I guess it's all in my head. Usually if one of us has a problem, we speak to each other about it."

TWENTY-TWO

Am I a fool

We entered his room. "Even if the problem is related to one of you?" he asked.

That concerned me. "Actually, I never looked at it that way."

The dim light revealed a very good-looking little place. Yoann had decorated the walls with pareus and pictures of all the clubs he'd worked. "This is a really nice place you have here."

He retorted, "Louise, you haven't told me what you think about me yet." He turned my face toward him. Hot chills moved through my body like a fever, but I had to keep it together.

"Neither have you," I replied with a smile while looking in his eyes. At that minute, I said to myself, *I should have listened to my little voice.* But then again, maybe I didn't want to listen to it. Maybe this was exactly what I was waiting for.

He placed his arms around my waist and then slowly rested his lips against mine. He kissed me on my lips, my neck, and my chest over and over again. His hand moved up from my waist to my breasts, where he started unbuttoning my blouse. He moved slowly and tentatively until I was revealed to him. Then I felt his warm hand moving on my stomach, caressing me lightly. His worm hand moved upward toward my breast ever so slowly, caressing each one and bringing them to a peak until I had only one thing on my mind. I knew this was it for me and help was never coming, not even from the voice in my head. I wanted him to make love to me.

He lifted me up in his arms to lay me on his bed, where he continued to slowly and sensually take off every piece of my clothing. In no time, he stripped down to nothing, and finally we lay close to each other. His body felt so warm against mine. I could feel his every muscle play under my caressing hand. He took me in his embrace, and I lost myself in him. He seemed to pick me up from the earth and bring me toward the clouds, where my mind lost track of every bit of reality.

I must have fallen asleep because when I did open my eyes again, Yoann was asleep next to me, one arm lazily resting on my stomach. My watch said it was 5:30 a.m. I couldn't believe time had flown by so quickly. I looked back at Yoann. In his sleep, he looked like a little child, which was quite a change from the last few hours, where he'd showed me he was more than a virile man. Those hours of love would always stay in my memory. He was such a sweet and attentive lover. I felt so light in my head. I quickly got up, dressed, and then gave Yoann a light kiss before leaving the room.

While walking back to my room, I knew I was mentally and physically disturbed, drained, and out of control. The only help I would ever be able to get again was from me. A part of me trembled during the walk back to my room, but my legs got me home safely. Deep inside, I didn't feel safe, just out of control and lost.

Morning was about to arrive when I walked into my room. I didn't want Andrea to know I'd slept out. Not yet. To my surprise, Andrea was not in her bed. I was so sleepy that all I dreamed about was to lying in my bed and sleeping, even though I wondered where she was. I thought of taking a shower before slipping into my bed, but I wanted to sleep with Yoann's manly smell on me. As soon as I put my head on the pillow, I slipped into a dreamless sleep.

TWENTY-THREE

The morning after

I woke up with a pep in my step, a pain on one side of my ass, and a crotch on fire. Boy, was I in trouble. I was hooked on Yoann, my black beauty. After slowly limping around the room, the pain in my ass went away, but not the thoughts in my mind. It must have been that cramp in my butt that had me wired to think that way. I wanted to cry, but I didn't because I understood I was on my own. *Where is help when you need it the most? Especially when you cannot cry out?* I remembered walking back to my bed, before going blank.

It wasn't until noon, that I opened my eyes again. Andrea had been in the room while I was still sleeping, because on her bed there was a change of clothes lying in a heap as if she was in a hurry to leave the room. I reluctantly got up from my warm, comfy bed to slip into the shower. As the warm water flowed over my head and down my body, I wondered, how I could have broken all of my moral principles and allowed someone I didn't even know into my private space. I knew it was that little voice in my head haunting me, but it was much too late. I used the shower to hide my tears as I wondered what love was, and where love was. Was I loved, or was I simply a fool like most blondes? I wanted to believe love was blind, but that little voice in my head told me otherwise. Love may be blind, but it could still see in the dark.

At that point, my stomach made me realize I was hungry. At twelve thirty, I left the room to get me some lunch. I was holding it together. As usual, the buffet was filled with so much variety that it was hard to make up my mind. I was so hungry, it was unbelievable. While eating, thoughts of Andrea coursed through my mind. I wondered why I had this feeling she was avoiding me. Knowing her, I didn't think she would do a thing like that, but I could never be sure. I left the dining room and decided on making a short stop at my room to see whether Andrea was there.

When I opened the door, I found her sitting and staring out through the window of the porch. I could tell she wasn't admiring the ocean view. She seemed lost in some kind of battle inside her mind, just like me. As a matter of fact, I startled her when I came in. "Oh, it's you, Louise. I didn't expect to see you at this time." She avoided my eyes for a reason I couldn't quite understand.

"Are you all right, Andrea?" I inquired, worried at her weird attitude these last few days. At that moment, Yoann's words came back to my mind. *Even if this problem is related to one of you?* Then I wondered whether I wasn't the reason for her weird attitude.

After a moment of hesitation, Andrea came out with it. "Louise, I have to admit something to you." That note struck a vein in my leg, and I started nibbling away on a fingernail as she went on. "I know I have been acting foolish with you in the last day or so. Right now, I came to terms with myself about something that concerns you." After another moment of hesitation, she continued. "And Yoann."

My heart skipped two beats, my fingernail was down to nil, and I wondered whether I needed to use the toilet first, but now was a bad time. I sighed and fumbled my words. "What do you mean? What did I do?"

"It isn't something you did purposefully or intentionally. It's just that I was jealous of you being with Yoann and him preferring you to me. I was mad at you for your beauty, your charm, or whatever attracted him to you instead of me. I know how foolish it sounds now, but I somehow hated you in a certain way, and right now I feel ashamed of this. You see, I really like him a lot, or so I believed until yesterday night. I became close to Devin—you know, the other bartender. If it wasn't for him, I think I would not be talking to you like this right now. Devin is so sweet and understanding, and he makes me see into myself like no one has ever done before. He helped me to understand that this vacation place is like a paradise out of a dream, and that Yoann was a part of that dream that I will be leaving behind to go back to my reality. It's only when he made me see it under that light that I understood my feelings.

"And as you already know, I did not come back to sleep here last night. Of course, that helped too. I'm not saying that I fell in love with Devin, but he was there at the right time, I guess, and I like him dearly for it. Louise, I'm so sorry for what I did to you. Can you forgive me?"

I nodded and cried, closed the space that separated us, and took her in my arms. "My god, Andrea, I had no idea. Of course I forgive you, even though I had no idea of the extent of your behavior in the last few days." I knew I needed all the help in the world, and her listening ear was at my mercy. "I'll tell you frankly, after hearing you out, I don't know whether I should be thinking like you concerning Yoann. It is true we are here on vacation, and everything here seems to come straight out of a dream. I only hope that Yoann is not part of this dream and that when the time comes to wake up from it, he will disappear. I wouldn't want our relationship to change, and that's why I'm a bit afraid of what the outcome will be."

"I guess I understand what you mean. But only time will tell you that." She put on her bathing suit, pleased with the outcome of our talk. "What would you say we head to the beach and laze around a while?"

"Sounds good to me." I sat on the porch, waiting for her.

"Guess what happened to me yesterday night?" she went on while undressing.

"What?"

"Well, you know I was hanging out with Devin. We danced the night away at the disco. When we left to go to his room, I had this feeling David was following us. I just hope nothing comes out of it. As of now, I haven't seen him around."

"Well, I hope so too. Do you like David?" I asked her calmly.

She hadn't changed her mind. "I told you before, he's a fool. As a friend, yes, but that's all there is to it for now, nothing more."

When Andrea said, "He's a fool," my heart jumped because I knew the only fool was me. I was happy Andrea had expressed her true feelings toward me, but I was still afraid to tell her everything. I even forgot I needed to use the ladies' room. I came from a family of all boys, so I learned to suppress some of my feelings, but it eventually caught up to me.

"David is a very sympathetic fellow. But I don't wish to make love with him, and that's exactly what he seems to be looking for with me," Andrea continued.

"And you're not in love with Devin either."

"I'll tell you frankly. Right now, I don't know with whom I'm in love. If my boyfriend back home could hear and see me now, I wouldn't live to see another vacation." We both laughed at that statement. How true it was for both of us.

We made our way out. "You know, Andrea, this place has made me see a whole new side to life that could never exist in our city life. I guess Yoann is a great part of this new vision, hey? Are you falling in love with him, my dear?"

I looked at her and flashed her my best smile. "You'd better believe it, like I've never felt before. I can't explain how, because words are not enough to describe the depth of it."

"My, my, aren't we mysterious. Is it the same for him?" she asked.

"To tell you the truth, I don't really know. We haven't talked about it in so many words. I just go by the feelings he projects to me. I feel I could put trust in him no matter what. I hope you understand." I was not planning to admit it, but the position I was verbally placed in made me yield and submit.

"Don't tell me. You would be ready to accept him being here while you go back home to wait for him, and you wouldn't wonder about him, be jealous, or anything of that sort. Am I right?" Her flawless words punished my heart.

"Maybe that's what I mean. I cannot be 100 percent sure. After all, I only met the guy a few days ago. But still, I'm sure it could be done."

"No, sugar pie. It could be tried," she concluded.

I said nothing.

We walked on the beach while talking about other things, and then we took lounge chairs and made ourselves comfortable. We chatted a while longer until the sailing regatta started, and Andrea decided to join it. I stayed on the lounge chair, taking in the sun for what would probably be the last time. Time sure flew by fast! I wished this vacation would never end and didn't feel like going back home. Maybe it was all because of Yoann. After all, I sure didn't want to leave him now, and the beauty and the peacefulness surrounding was incredible. I would never find this back home. I felt much better after talking to Andrea, but I needed a drink. I made my way to the beach bar, knowing that I would see Yoann, which made me feel very good.

TWENTY-FOUR

Alain and David emotion

As I entered the beach bar, I bumped into Alain. It looked like he had been waiting for me. "Hello, Alain," I told him cheerfully.

"I would like to speak to you. Would you mind stepping outside?" His face registered contained emotions as he led the way out. I wondered what the scene was about. I tried to figure out what in the hell I had done for him to act this way toward me; he looked very angry. We finally reached a spot that satisfied him, so he stopped and looked at me. "I was up by your room twice last night to see you. Now, if you don't care about me, let me know, but please don't lead me on. Maybe you think you're too good for me, but don't lie to me about a boyfriend you have back home when it's really because you like somebody else here. Just say so!"

He was obviously furious. So that was his problem. I wished I could tell him. I had to admit that seeing it from that angle, it sounded as if I really had lied to him. I knew I would be wasting my time trying to explain, especially given his furious condition. I did feel a little guilty, but I still felt he had no right to meddle in my personal life. "What are you talking about, Alain?" I said, playing as if I didn't know.

"Up front," he said. "I am talking about you and Yoann."

"What about us? We're only friends."

"Do you call walking out of his room at five thirty in the morning being only friends? Do you think I am a fool?"

"Please don't say that," I interjected, thinking that his words matched my own.

He went on. "It's my job to know what goes on in this village."

I knew I needed to calm him, so I said, "Alain, Yoann is only a friend of mine. I was at his place all right, but only for a while. I fell asleep at his place. That's why I left so late. Can you understand that?"

He calmly said, "And you really expect me to believe that?"

"No, Alain. That's up to you to decide."

"I guess you trust him more than you trust me, right?" he said with a cynical smile playing at the corner of his mouth.

I was having enough problems of my own, and I sure didn't need more. "Listen. I would like you to stop acting so childish. Try to be reasonable. I did not promise you anything. As a matter of fact, you know straight and plain that I didn't feel the same way about you. And as for Yoann, well, it just happened that way."

It took a while for him to answer me back. "You know Louise, I really like you, but you are blind to lose out." With that said, he walked away.

I couldn't see how I had led him on. I made my way into the beach bar to unload my feelings, mixed as they were, on poor Yoann, who greeted me cheerfully. "Hey, there you are, my dear! You're looking good this afternoon." He gave me a quick kiss on my lips. That brought a big smile to my face and made me feel less of a bad girl. I knew he had seen Alain and me outside.

"I guess you saw Alain and me. Tell me, how do you suppose Alain found out that I slept in your room last night?"

"Well, let's see. What time did you leave my place?"

"It was about five thirty."

"And did you see anyone along the way?"

"I spotted Patrick as I walked out, but he was so busy kissing that girl, so he couldn't possible have seen me."

"Honey, do you know who Patrick is?"

"He's in charge of scuba diving."

"Yes, but he's also Alain's best friend. Now, does that answer your question?"

My expression fell. "Well, some people should mind their own goddamned business!" That piece of information pissed me off. Some people liked to spread rumors and make trouble.

"Hey, Louise, don't look so hostile. Cheer up a little. Don't let all this foolishness get to you. What would you say if I offered you a fresh pina colada?"

He sounded so warm and relaxed, so eager to appease my mood. I had no other choice but to smile and agree with him. "That would be great. Thank you, Yoann."

He turned to mix it and then returned to me. While handing it over, he explained, "Tonight, I have to be part of the award ceremony for the sport day. It's followed by a cocktail party, If you plan to attend, you won't be sorry. The cocktail party is every Friday, and people can never get enough. The cocktails are arranged quite skillfully across many tables draped in white and a few colors. It's a beautiful sight to see."

"I guess I'll have to be there."

"Good! Anyway, I want to ask you if I can see you afterward."

I sucked that pina colada down like water and then cleared my throat. "Well, why don't you have dinner with Andrea and me tonight?" I suggested. "We patched up our little misunderstanding, and I'm sure she would be delighted if you accepted." What else could I have said? I had to try to save my friendship with Andrea. After all, we were like sisters.

"Come to think of it, Louise, you two should eat together tonight. You must have a lot to make up for."

"Did you know you were the subject of our litigation?"

"I had an idea, ever since I had dinner with her."

"How did you guess?"

"It's easy for a man to know when a woman likes him. It was obvious by the way she spoke and looked at me that night. It gave her away."

I was surprised to hear the news from his own lips, and I just had to ask. "Was it the same way with me?"

"To tell you the truth, it was a little different. Why don't we keep it a mystery? Because not everything can be explained in words. Now, I'll see you sometime after dinner, all right? Don't worry—I'll find you wherever you are. You'll have to excuse me—I have business to attend to." On that, he kissed my nose like before and went behind the bar.

I had always been in control of my relationships, but that was not so with Yoann. I lost it from the time I first met him. It was the most uncertain feeling a women could have. Was that foolish? Still I wondered. *Am I a fool, or someone searching to know herself? How can someone speak one thing, the truth, and do the opposite? Am I not a liar? Truly I am not! They say life is a learning process. But if that is so, my hurt and my pain have just begun.* How I wished someone could hear my silent cry.

I returned to the beach to find David lying in a lounge chair next to mine. Andrea hadn't gotten back from the sailing regatta. I lay down in my chair to find that David was in need of a sympathetic ear. He told me how much he was in love with Andrea for the next hour. It was a good thing I had asked him if it was any bother to him if I closed my eyes—because of the sun, I told him. At least I didn't have to pretend too much that I was listening. Poor David was as broken as I was. The only difference was how each of us was dealing with it.

It was four thirty when I sat up, collected my belongings, said goodbye to David, and headed to the main bar. I had a brilliant idea. I would pick up a champagne bucket filled with ice and two glasses to bring up to the room, and I'd put our bottle of champagne in the ice to cool and surprise Andrea.

TWENTY-FIVE

The Surprise feeling like a million dollars

I reached the room with the glasses and ice and arranged them nicely on the little table in the porch. The champagne on the table and the overlooking view of the ocean and the village was picture-perfect. I turned around and headed to the bathroom for a shower. As I got out of the shower and reached for the doorknob, the bathroom door burst open. "Surprise!" Andrea yelled, handing me a glass of champagne.

"You little devil. You scared me! I didn't even hear you come in." I took the glass from her and smiled with delight.

"Louise, you had a wonderful idea to chill that bottle of champagne. It's funny because I was just thinking of that bottle on my way here. Talk about coincidence!"

With my towel around me, we walked back to the table "Shall we make a toast?" I picked up the bottle to refill our glasses.

"To friendship, and to our happiest vacation," she said, touching my glass. We smiled warmly at each other as we sat talking and laughing over champagne, and time flew by so fast.

At seven, Andrea jumped out of her chair. "My god! Look at the time, and I haven't even shower yet." She rushed into the shower in order to be ready for the award ceremony at seven thirty. I decided to wear my best silk outfit to match my champagne mood, and Andrea also decided to dress stunningly. At seven twenty-five we made our way out of the room, laughing and feeling like a million dollars. Arm in arm, we headed to the small amphitheater, where we were delighted by the beautiful sight. Yoann was true to his word: it was magnificent. Table after table was dressed with pyramids of glasses of all different styles filled with colorful cocktails. At the foot of each pyramid, exotic cocktails ensconced in pineapple, grapefruit, or coconuts were awaiting on the most refined plates. We barely had time to take our seats before the ceremony started. The whole sport team was on the dance floor to give out the awards from the Olympics day and other activities. We were more than surprised to be given a medal for the best sand sculpture.

After the awards ceremony, the chief of village came on the microphone to begin a wonderful presentation of cocktails from around the world, where GSs dressed as dancers from different countries to present a piece of folkloric dance. Each dancing couple then presented a cocktail to people in the audience. It was interesting and so colorful, and at last the invitation was given for everyone to come and share a cocktail or two from the exquisitely arranged tables. At that announcement, GSs from the bar uncorked champagne bottles. They poured into the first glass on the top of a pyramid, and by the way they were all set, not one drop fell on the table but instead filled each and every glass like magic.

People moved toward the tables to get a sip of those fascinating cocktails. We mingled with the crowd; speaking here and there to people we'd met through the week. For most vacationers, it was like a farewell cocktail party because most were leaving the next day. Andrea and I tasted each other's drinks and then managed to leave the dance floor with glasses of champagne—to continue in the same vein, we told ourselves with a giggle.

We went up to the restaurant. Food had become an urgent matter in order to keep our sanity after all the champagne. We were delighted to discover that it was a candlelit dinner with full service. We were automatically seated and enjoyed our champagne while chatting and getting to know our fellow diners. That night was the most exquisite dinner we'd had, even though all the food had been exquisite at the club. We left the table sated.

On our way to the main bar, we spotted Cenny, still sitting on his good luck bench. "Hey, girls! Come on over," he said loudly. We made our way toward him. "Ladies, you sure look lovely tonight." His eyes inspected us from head to toe.

"Cenny, tell me, why do you always sit on this bench top?" Andrea asked him.

"So that I can see everything passing by. That way I'm sure I don't miss anything. See? I didn't miss you!"

"Is Devin working tonight?" Andrea asked him.

"Why? Is he your boyfriend?" he asked, giving her a quizzical look.

"No, I would just like to know, that's all." She smiled at his funny face.

"Don't lie now, girl. Remember I'm an Indian, and Indians can smell very well. And right now, you smell barman!" As he said it, he started sniffing very loudly, and his face gave such a funny, expression that we burst out laughing.

"Cenny, how long have you been working for the club?" I wanted to know how they managed to endure him.

"Too long!" he replied swiftly.

"Please be serious, Cenny. For once," I replied.

"Okay. Twelve years and two months."

"Twelve years? Why so long?" Andrea seemed amazed by that.

"Because I enjoy what I do—simple."

"You must be the one-in-a-million GS, staying for so long."

He replied, "Once there were many like me, but now I don't think so."

"This is a very nice life you all have here. I wish I could be a part of it too. The GS here are all so talented," Andrea said.

"We all do our best for everyone."

Chatting with Cenny was very refreshing. We kept him company until the dance floor started at nine thirty. We did all we could to drag Cenny to dance with us a while, but to no avail. We had no other choice but to let him be. We excused ourselves because there was nothing in the world that would have kept us from dancing that night.

I felt much better about myself. Maybe it was because of all the ongoing excitement, and that little voice in my head had fallen asleep.

TWENTY-SIX

The Disco, in the arms of love

While we walked back to the disco for a few dance before turning in, Yoann came out of nowhere, frightening us a little. "Hello, girls. You weren't expecting me, but here I am. How about going to the disco for a while?" He was delicate enough to not kiss me in front of Andrea, and I was very grateful for that.

"That's exactly where we were going, you know," I answered him, smiling gently.

We were not inside the disco for more than three minutes before Andrea was grabbed by a jubilant Devin and dragged onto the dance floor. Yoann and I remained standing near the bar. Alain approached and asked me to dance, and I obliged. "Excuse me, Yoann. I'll be only a few minutes."

When Alain asked me to dance, he had taken the liberty of holding my hand, and as I followed, he continued to hold it tightly. At that point, I pulled my hand away. We began to dance, but he kept pressing his body against mine, and I became uncomfortable. "Will I be able to see you later?" he asked me very seriously.

"I don't think so, Alain," I answered a bit condescendingly.

"Well, be sure to let me know when you are sure," he replied contemptuously. I simply looked at him with a tight smile. We danced a few more uncomfortable minutes, and then he suddenly said, "Thanks for the dance." He turned on his heel and was gone.

I thought, *Let me get back to interesting matters.* I couldn't help myself, and my legs returned me to Yoann.

He exclaimed, "I really like the way you dance. It's a real pleasure for me to watch you."

"Thank you, but listen. Could we please get out of here? This place is a little too stuffy all of a sudden."

"Yes, of course." His eyes roamed the place and rested on Alain, who stood near the entrance of the disco. He then took my hand and led me out through the back door. I didn't even have time to inform Andrea of our sudden departure. "There is no mistaking that Alain really likes you. By the way he looks at you, his intentions are written all over his face."

"Yes, and he's really pushing it. I don't like the way his remarks sound. Tell me, Yoann. Do most of the GSs have new girlfriends every week?"

"No, not all of them. Some do, but it's just like at any other place. As long as you have people coming together, it's unavoidable."

"And what about you?" I looked deep into his eyes when I asked that question.

"I shouldn't answer that."

"And why not?"

"Whatever I say, if you have it in your mind that one GS is bad, all of them will look bad to you. Do you really think my saying no would make you believe me?"

He had a way with words, so I insisted. "Maybe it would help me to understand why I fell in love with you so quickly—and why I feel I've known you all my life. I feel I can put a lot of trust in you."

"And is something wrong with that?" he asked.

"No, I guess not, but I don't really know much about you, Yoann."

We walked in the direction of his room. "I think you know me well," he said as we approached his door.

"What do you mean, I know you well?"

"What type of person did you think I was?"

We entered his room, and that smell of his I love so much weakened me before I answered. "I thought you were a very nice and honest man, always eager to please"

"And were you right up to now?"

We moved closer to his bed, and I answered. "Yes, but I still think it takes time to know someone more deeply."

He gently placed both of his hand in mine. "Do you need more time to know me?" he asked, staring into my eyes as his lips came closer to mine.

"Yes," I whispered.

"Then take all the time you need," he whispered back before kissing me. There was something about the way he kissed me that turned me on and made me lose control over myself. His touch was so soft and gentle, and his skin under my hand felt like the skin of a baby. He slowly undressed me while his hands gently caressed my sensitive skin. "You feel so soft," he whispered in my ears while nibbling my earlobe.

He picked me up in his arms and slowly placed me on his bed. We undressed, and then he made love to me until we both felt we couldn't breathe anymore. We fell into an exhausted, dreamless sleep.

TWENTY-SEVEN

The next morning

The next morning when I woke up, Yoann had already left. It was ten thirty. I slowly got out of bed and went into his shower. This time, there were no tears to wash away, and the only regret was having to leave his room. That little voice in my head never woke up, so I knew I was on my own.

By the time I left the room, it was eleven. I made a stop at my room to make a quick change, and when I entered, I met Andrea and Devin sitting in bed and playing a game of chess. "Good morning, you two! How's life?"

"Morning," they both answered.

"By the way," Andrea went on, "last night David and Andrew were looking for you. They wanted to say goodbye, so they asked me to deliver the message. 'Goodbye, nice meeting you.' There, now you know." To Devin she said, "Check."

"Oh, you!" he shouted playfully.

I grabbed my pareu and bathing suit, made my way to the bathroom, changed, and was ready to go. "What are you two planning to do today?"

"We'll finish this chess game and have lunch. I don't really know after that. We'll see what time brings." At that, Andrea returned her attention to the game.

"I'm going to walk a little on the beach. I'll see you at lunch," I said as I left the room.

The sun shone brightly, but its warmth was cooled by the fresh ocean breeze. I had many things to think about. So much had happened in such a short time, and I had to sort things out. I wanted Yoann to be a part of my life, but it seemed so impossible. I remembered the words Alain had told me that first night when he had tried to kiss me: "What happens in the club stays in the club." I didn't want to look at it that way because what I felt was more than just a fling romance on another beautiful vacation. It was much more. And to think that in two days, I would have to leave and go back to … what? Not much.

My boyfriend back home was a nice guy, and I liked him a lot, but I was not in love with him. I never had been in love with him. I continued walking and thinking, and when I lifted my eyes from the sandy beach, I found myself a few feet from the beach bar, with Yoann comfortably seated and gazing at me. "I wasn't expecting to see you here so soon." When he talked, his smile never left his face.

"I hope you're not too disappointed!" I said teasingly.

"Oh no, on the contrary. Come and sit with me for a while. I don't really have anything to do for now." He brought a chair for me to sit on. "I saw that you seemed to be pondering a great deal on the beach. Is there something bothering you?" he asked, concerned.

"Well, not really bothering me. I was thinking about this place, you, and everything that has happened since I got here. Most of all, I'm thinking about the way things have changed for me since I met you. Tell me, Yoann. Where do most GSs go at the end of each season?"

"Many go back home. Some go on vacation in another club or with friends, or they visit the country they're in. It really depends what one wants."

"And you? Where will you go?"

At that question, he looked at me for a while before answering. "I would love to see you again. That is, if that's what you want."

"Oh, Yoann. I wouldn't want it any other way." His words touched me dearly. I wanted to reach out and hug him to me, but instead, words came out of my mouth before I could stop them. "Do you believe in love?"

"Why do you ask me this question?" He looked at me in that analytical way that was so special to him.

I had to think a minute before answering. "Because after living in a paradise like this and seeing so many new faces each week, how could it be possible in so short a time to love someone?"

"Do you believe I love you?" he asked.

"Well, I know you care a lot for me," I replied.

"You're right about that. I do care a lot about you—very much indeed. But you see, for me love means caring, sharing, and succeeding in it. I wouldn't say I love you, because for me, love is not an earthly matter. It comes directly from the eternal to us, and from us to the eternal. Love comes from one's soul, and if your soul is eternal, so is love. For any human being, I can only care with all my heart. This is my own belief. You don't have to agree with it, but you'd have to accept it. Now, if you don't mind, I am starving. What would you say we head toward the restaurant?"

His words stunned me, but as I went over them in my mind, they made sense. This guy amazed me more with each passing day. I had never met someone with so much wisdom and understand. On our way, we were both silent, absorbed in our own thoughts.

The restaurant was less crowded, and we met up with Andrea and Devin around the buffet. We all sat together, talking and exchanging jokes. It was great because it was time Andrea and I were both with men we cared for. Unfortunately, Yoann and Devin had to leave us to attend a departure, so we finished lunch on our own.

We made our way out of the restaurant, and just as we passed the usual place where Cenny always sat, I poked Andrea in the ribs. "Let's sit here a while. I would love to see what Cenny finds so attractive about it."

Andrea agreed, and we sat. "Comfy," she said, nodding to herself. "But let's go before he comes back."

In a matter of seconds, we heard Cenny's voice crying out. "Hey! Hey, you two! Don't you know you must pay to sit there?"

"Ha! We already paid our fare," Andrea said, laughing.

"So how are you doing, girls?"

"Great, and how about you, Cenny?" I said sweetly.

"Great also, but I miss my bench!" he said with pursed lips, looking ready to cry.

"We are keeping it warm for you," Andrea replied with a smile.

"Don't worry, we were only passing through. We were on our way to the swimming pool. Right, Andrea? So we'll see you later," I said without waiting for Andrea's answer.

"Take care now," he told us, taking his position. "I also have a good view of the swimming pool area!" he added with a big grin on his face. We smiled back.

The sun was hot, so we decided to find a shady spot. It was good to do nothing but relax. Andrea's voice broke the silence enveloping us. "Oh, how I wish I could take Devin home with me, but I don't know whether he would be able to escape from this paradise for long. Everything needed is in this place. Last night, he told me he wanted to see me again."

"When we first arrived here, I thought you liked Paul."

"Yes, I do like Paul. And David too. But they are so similar—the macho type. Women don't mean much to them, except when it comes to bedtime fun. I bet they have a different girlfriend every week or so. I don't know. I only know I couldn't love a man who thinks that way. They may be good in bed, but out of bed, they wouldn't know how to love a woman."

After hearing her, I could only say, "I guess you're right. You know, when I think about Yoann, I would like to know what makes me love him. Why not Alain? They are both nice and kind to me. Well, Alain was once. It's something I can't put my finger on that attracts me to Yoann. Anyhow, would you like to join me for a workout?"

Surprised to hear that, she said, "Louise, what kind of workout are you talking about?"

"A little weight lifting. What did you think?" I replied, laughing heartily at her funny expression.

"You go in the gym. I think I'm gonna pass on that. And anyway, I'm supposed to meet Devin. We were planning on sailing this afternoon."

We stayed a short while, enjoying the cool shade before going our separate ways, me going to the exercising room and Andrea going with Devin to the sailing shack. I felt really good about myself.

TWENTY-EIGHT

The unexpected

hen I entered the weight lifting room, I noticed a guy working on the universal machine. At first glance, he looked familiar. When I glanced a second time, I recognized him: Alain! Right then, my heartbeat started pumping a little faster. It crossed my mind to turn around and leave the room, but it was already too late—he'd spotted me. I opted for the nice, "there's no problem" attitude. "Hello there, Alain. I didn't know you enjoyed weight lifting."

He stared at me for a while without saying a word, and then he continued with his exercises. I felt very uncomfortable; the air in the place seemed to be frozen in place. However, I decided to try the weights. I didn't know what else to say to him.

Right then, he stopped exercising and approached me. "You know, I shouldn't even be talking to you after the way you treated me," he said, giving me a hard look.

"Alain, I'm sorry if I—" I didn't have the chance to continue.

"You're sorry? Oh, I don't think so! You know, I believed in you at first, but women like you only deserve to be led on like you led me on. I offered to love you! Anybody else might simply take you for granted. How could you tell me you didn't want to sleep with me—and then let Yoann screw you? You think he's better than me because he's bigger and stronger and has a better body? Or is it that you'd rather be making love to one like him? Why can't you understand when somebody cares for you? Please, Louise, don't make me hate myself—or you."

I could see the tears in his eyes, but there was nothing more I could do because as I saw it, we were both in the same position. The only difference was how one dealt with it, and I was truly having problems dealing with my personal issues.

I was getting upset by this fool of a man who thought everything had to come his way, as if he deserved every and all things in this world. His words had lit a fire that was not about to be put out easily, and I called it like I saw it. "Now, you just wait a minute, buster! Who the hell do you think you are to talk to me as if you own me or something? Let me tell you, Mister Sadness, that I don't owe you anything—nothing at all! If your big head plays trick on you and makes you believe words and actions I didn't do, it is not my problem. And as for Yoann and me, that is of no concern to you! Your jealousy is twisting events so badly in your head, and you believe in them so strongly, that I think you're blind. I am so disappointed in you. What do you think I am, a one-night stand, or something you can use at your convenience? Come back to earth, little boy, because you just knocked on the wrong door! I thought we had a nice friendship going, but I see with your crooked mind, it won't lead us anywhere." I made a motion as if to leave.

Alain took hold of my hand, a stunned expression on his face. I stopped to hear him out. "Louise, all I want is you—to show you how I feel about our relationship." His voice had softened.

I replied, "I don't call sleeping with you friendship, Alain. It is something I can't believe in with you, and nothing you say or do will make me change my mind. For what it's worth, when you love someone, you never speak to the person that way."

"Do you call sleeping with Yoann friendship?" he asked, jealousy flashing in his eyes.

I said to myself, *The idiot just changed my words and fired them back at me. So silly.* It was eating him up that I was with Yoann. I was disgusted, and I said. "That's very different, and also none of your business. How can I make you understand that?"

"You say you care about Yoann, but you don't even know him! I offered for you to get to know me, but instead you'd rather make a fool out of me."

"No, Alain, that's not true. I didn't come here looking for anyone to fall in love with. But I care very much about Yoann. I could even say I am falling in love with him. It is something that happened, but I did not plan for it to happen. You are pushing me to love you, but don't you understand that things don't always work out. You can't force things on people, least of all love."

I felt my eyes tingling from tears, and then to my surprise, he blamed me by uttering, "One thing I've learned from you is hate." He turned from me and back to the universal weight lifting machine. After taking hold on the crossbar, he pumped the weights like a man fueled with energy. For a minute I was impressed, but as fast as he started, he abruptly and unexpected ended, and he gasped for air. Breathing heavily, he added, "I don't want to say I hate you for what you did to me."

Again I interjected. "Stop, Alain. I have to explain. I don't want to lose a friendship, and I don't want you to hate me. I had no plans to hurt you, believe me." But as I talked, I knew I was wasting my time. He already had in his mind that I had done him wrong.

"Yeah, sure. You really think Yoann loves you, don't you? But I know he doesn't. He should be glad he got you in his bed. I wasn't so lucky."

I thought, *I'm lucky no one is in the weight lifting room to hear his foolishness.* Then I said, "I've about had enough of this nonsense! I thought we could be friends, but I see you don't want that at all. It's a shame." I stormed out the room.

I went straight up to my room and threw myself onto the bed, rerunning the afternoon's events in my head. I must have fallen asleep because I was awoken by a familiar hand caressing my back and hips with a soft, tender stroke. I turned over to make sure I wasn't dreaming. "Yoann! What are you doing here?" I asked surprised but happy to see him. I looked at my watch and saw it was six thirty. "I mean, how did you know I was here?"

"I didn't. I just came to see if you were, and here you are! I met Alain a little earlier. He came to me with one hell of a question."

"Oh," I said. "I saw him at the weight lifting room, and we had quite an argument. I was really angry at him then, but I guess now I kind of understand his reaction. What did he ask you?"

"He wanted to know whether I was sleeping with you."

"And what did you tell him?"

"I told him you had slept at my place all night, but we didn't make love."

"Why did you lie?" I asked.

"*Lie* is a strong word. What I did was give him what he wanted and needed to hear. Now, if he believes me, it wouldn't surprise me if he approaches you differently and tries his luck once more. But he's not a bad guy. I'm sure he will be very civilized."

I wondered for a minute what Yoann had really said to him. "For one thing, he's very jealous of your body."

"Anybody who works on his body could attain a build like mine. If he doesn't do it, he'll always be envious of others."

"That's more than true. I think he's already started working on it."

"I hope you're right, for his sake. Now, would you like to meet me at the main bar around eight o'clock? We can have dinner."

"Eight it is."

He quickly kissed me, and said, "See you then, good-looking," and made his way out.

I entered the shower, singing at the top of my lungs to Chris de Burg's "Lady in Red," when I heard a commotion in the room. The cassette player was turned off, and a screaming Andrea made her way inside the bathroom as I put a towel around my body.

"Louise, Louise! My god, guess who I just ran into this afternoon? You won't believe your ears, I tell you! I was so stunned to see him. Boy, the world is small!"

"Andrea, please calm down. Now, tell me who this wonder guy is?"

"You remember Gregory, my first boyfriend after we left school? Well, he just arrived in Playa. I couldn't believe it at first! We both noticed each other right away."

"Didn't he get married sometime last year?"

"Yeah, he did, but he's divorced now. Only stayed married three months. I knew he wasn't the marring type. He had too many girlfriends to get used to being with only one. He's thinner, but his face hasn't changed a bit. He told me it wasn't his first time in the club. He only vacations in the club—as he said, it's the only way to go."

"There is one thing I can say about Gregory now," I said, smiling. "He's always where the action is." We both agreed and laughed at the remark, remembering long ago stories about him.

"He invited me to dinner, but I told him I was already busy. I told him you were also here. He can't wait to see you."

"Oh, I'm sure we'll run into each other sometime tonight."

We both got ready for dinner, taking great pain to look our best. Before eight fifteen, we finally made our way down to the restaurant. "Louise, have you noticed blondes are given no preference here? None at all!" Andrea whispered to me.

"Yeah, I noticed that too. But you have to admit everyone here is so unique and so different."

"You've got that right," she said, raising her voice.

Yoann and Devin were standing around the empty bar, waiting patiently for us. The minute they saw us, their faces lit up with smiles. "You sure are lovely to look at, girls," they said almost in unison.

We had a marvelous dinner. After dinner, Yoann and I went down to the bar for cognacs, and then we relaxed near the pool and waited the night show. Yoann had to participate in the show, so he left me early in order to get ready.

Twenty-nine

Meting Gregory

As I walked back toward the main bar, I was accosted from behind by none other than Gregory, the old boyfriend of Andrea's. "Well, if it isn't Louise! My god! You're more beautiful than I remember. How have you been doing all these years?" We hugged, and he kissed both my cheeks in a very friendly manner.

"Gregory! You sure gave us a surprise! So how are you doing?"

"I'm always in top shape—you should remember that! And always ready to party!"

"The more I talk to you, the more I can see you haven't changed."

"Baby, that's what makes life interesting!"

We continued to chat and laugh at the bar over drinks, until it was showtime. He turned down my offer to join me for the show; instead, he went to meet some friends boozing tequila shots at the other side of the bar. I laughed at his recognizable behavior. He would never change.

When I walked to the amphitheater, I glanced at the back and saw Andrea waving her hand at me; she had reserved my seat. I figured Devin was also in the show because he was nowhere in sight. I took my seat just as the lights dimmed and the show started. Most of the show consisted of electing a "Mr. and. Mrs. Playa." The GSs selected a few couples from the audience and had them competing against one another in games that were funnier as the night went on. The show was followed by a complete GS presentation, all of them dressed in white and wearing Uncle Sam hats. It was charming. It finished with the crazy signs, like always, and then the eleven thirty dance floor began.

By the time we got out of the amphitheater, Yoann and Devin were already on the dance floor, along with almost all the GSs. I imagined it was to put everyone at ease and get people to dance. Upon seeing all those people on the dance floor already, even the shyest person would be tempted to go right on dancing. I made my way toward Yoann. Alain stood right behind him. I saw that he noticed me by looking over Yoann's shoulders, but I played as if I hadn't seen him. I wasn't really angry with Alain, just disappointed, but he made things so difficult and unexplainable that I didn't feel like arguing. Right then, I changed my mind, smiled at Yoann, and turned around, heading for the bar. I knew Yoann would follow me.

"You don't feel like dancing, Louise?"

"No, not really," I lied. "Not this song anyway. Would you like a drink?"

He called me on it. "Louise, is it really this song, or is it because of Alain?"

Denying it wouldn't have made a difference so I asserted my innocence. "A little of both. Does that answer your question?"

As I answered him, I noticed that Gregory was still at the other side of the bar. He looked very happy and unsteady. His friends were heavy drinkers, just like him.

"Would you like an Amaretto?" Yoann asked me, smiling.

"That will be fine." I hadn't had one in a long time.

Just then, Gregory started calling my name. "Louise! Louise, come on over. Hurry!" I excused myself and went to meet his friends. After he introduced me to his friends, he whispered to me, "Louise, you know how I go. We don't hide any secrets from each other."

Since when? I thought.

"Are you going out with that Samson over there?" he asked, pointing his finger at Yoann in a very obvious manner."

"Who, him? Oh, no, Gregory. You know I would never do a thing like that," I said sarcastically. It was none of his business anyway.

"Yes, but I also know you have special taste when it comes to your men, and the way I saw you two at dinner, it looks like he had you in the palm of his hand." I hated the way this guy described Yoann in a chauvinist manner.

"No, no, he's not quite my style, dear. This time you figured it all wrong. You see, he's not the one to retain my attention. He's only a good friend of mine. Now, why don't you tell me why you called me here in such a hurry?" I said, cutting short the foolish talk.

"Just to have a drink—or two or three. Why not? And meet my friends and have some fun. What's your rush?"

With him, I had to keep it simple and under control. "Gregory, I'm flattered you wanted my company, but I was already in conversation with 'that Samson' over there. So if you'll excuse me, I'll see you around." With that, I turned on my heels and went back to Yoann.

Yoann handed me my drink and asked me if everything was all right.

"Yes, don't worry. He's an old school friend who wanted to know more about me."

"In other words, another Alain." His words made me laugh because they were true.

"Would you like to go to the disco?" I asked him, wanting to change the subject.

"We could pass through, but I would really like to have an early night with you," he said, squeezing my hand a little tighter. I looked up at him and lost one breath, then two. I couldn't speak another word. That was exactly what we did. We entered the disco by the front door, and ten minutes later, we walked out the back and went directly to his room. I pushed any bad thoughts out of my mind. I didn't want it to spoil this night. I wanted it to be memorable.

THIRTY

Love is a hard lesson to be learnt

The next morning, I was awoken by Yoann's soft touch. Once again I felt my body responding to his demands. Nothing else mattered but us.

We lay in each other's arms with our eyes closed, lost in our own thoughts. Yoann had loved me that night like he had never loved me before, hungrily and never seeming to have enough, until we both fell asleep exhausted.

Alain's words came to my mind in a flash. *I offered to love you. Anyone else would use you.* For a fraction of a second, the thought came to my mind that maybe Yoann was using me after all. *No, he couldn't do that*, I told myself. The other little voice inside my head came back and asked me, *Why not?*

Well, because he seems so honest. It was true I didn't quite understand what he told me about not believing in any other love than the eternal, and how humans could only care for each other in this physical world, but they could not love because death was imminent. I simply knew that everything was all right, though I had no reason for that belief. It was a feeling, but it was so strong that I could have no doubts about it. Still, I had this urgency to ask him the question anyway.

"Yoann, I have something to ask you, but I want you to be more than honest with me. I hope you are not using me like so many others seem to be doing. You see, you haven't told me once that you love me or anything. Don't you know women need to be cuddled and told how much they are loved? At least once. So tell me, Yoann, do you love me only for my body, or is there more to it? I'm leaving anyway, so you don't have to spare me." I was becoming involved enough in my belief to sound a little angry in anticipation of the worst.

"Oh, no, please don't think of me in that way! I am absolutely not that type of man, believe me. It is true I haven't told you that I love you, but for me it is all a question of feelings. I feel your love for me; I don't have to hear it from your mouth. It is something that is there, and I can almost see it. For me, the word *love* has so many different meanings on earth. Not that I came from another planet, of course." He laughed and went on. "What I mean is that people were taught to say the word *love* for just about anything: I love spaghetti, I love my dog, I just fell in passionate love with this guy. But the next week, it's 'I hate this guy because I met another one, and I think I love him,' and so on. So you see, for me this word has no more meaning than it is given by the people, strange enough. But I will tell you something. I do care for you more than you will ever think, Louise. If it will make you feel better, yes, I do love you, my dear. And not only your body, but the whole you. I just can't see how I am going to make it when it's time for you to leave. I just hope I will be seeing you very, very soon." He started to tickle me and tease, which led to kissing, stroking, longing, and loving.

By nine thirty, Yoann had to leave the bed and headed to the shower in order to catch a quick breakfast before work at ten. I lazed around a while, taking in his surroundings. I wanted it imprinted inside my mind. I inhaled as much of his manly smell as I could to last me long enough until his return to me. I felt so happy yet so sad to know that our short love story was already coming to an end. I was so scared that without this chance to blossom into something strong, the feelings, the passion, the caring—I didn't know what to call it now—would cool off to nothingness. *Or maybe it will grow bigger and stronger by this separation,* I thought. I was so mixed up and had so little time left that I started to cry, and I couldn't stop myself. I was not in the shower to wash away my tears this time, and instead I cried myself back to sleep.

It wasn't until one fifteen that my eyes opened again. I couldn't believe I was sleeping away my last day in this paradise. I jumped out of bed and went straight to the shower. Once I got back to my room,

I jumped into my bathing suit and pareu. I left the room with a heart heavy with memories of the previous beautiful night, a light-footed walk, and a big smile that seemed stuck on my face. The surroundings of the village, the flowery garden, and the view in general still had the power to amaze me and make me wonder where all this beauty had disappeared to back home in New York. All was concrete and glass, and it was so cold that it made me shiver. With those thoughts, I promised myself to pass the afternoon capturing all this beauty on film. It was better than nothing, and I would use most of it to redecorate my room. With this in mind, I rushed to get changed and grab a quick lunch—or more accurately, what was left of lunch.

I stood on the beach, focusing my camera on the beautiful mountain scenery. I was just about to press the button when this funny face came in front of my picturesque setting. It was no other than Andrea, posing as if she were a model for a bikini advertisement. "Very funny!" I took the picture of her anyway.

"Where were you, Louise? I was looking all over for you this morning."

"I got up very late today, and I would think you know I spent the night at Yoann's."

"Well, yes, it did cross my mind, seeing as you weren't in this morning. So, how's life? Everything okay?" She looked concerned, knowing it was our last day in the village and how involved I was with Yoann.

"Yes, I feel fine—for now, at least."

"Oh, I wanted to tell you. We have to pass at the traffic office around five to collect our plane tickets, and then we must go to the bank to check out. Want to go together?"

"Great, but I'll have to meet you there. Right now, I'm just about finished taking my pictures, and I want to meet with Yoann until five."

Andrea said, "That's fine with me. I'm also meeting with Devin for a little tennis. See you later." And with that, she left.

I took a few more pictures of the surroundings, made sure to keep a few for Yoann, and headed toward the beach bar. A basketball game was taking place on the court, and Yoann was part of it. I sat on the grass in a sunny spot to watch the game while taking in some sun. It was another beautiful day, and like always, a light breeze came from the ocean, making the warmth bearable. It was a very exciting game, and they put in their best energies. All the players were soaked by the time the game was finished. Yoann's way of playing surprised me. I had no idea he could play so well.

He made his way toward me after the game, smiling and a little out of breath. "Did you enjoy the game?" he asked me.

"Well, yes, I did. Where did you learn to play so well?"

"Back in college, and with a lot of practice. I'm going to my room. Would you like to come?"

I was not sure how to answer, but my mouth knew. "Yeah, sure."

We headed toward his room, talking about his basketball tricks. As we entered his room, I took a seat on his bed and faced the bathroom. He entered the bathroom and started the shower, all the while taking to me. "I guess you're preparing to leave me tomorrow," he mentioned.

"How I wish I could stay longer, or even forever. But you know that's not possible. I may go back home, but a big part of me will stay behind here. I find that this is the best kind of life nature has to offer, but not all of us can have this life, Yoann."

"You know, I like the way you say my name. It sounds so sexy with your accent. Beautiful!" I knew he deliberately left the bathroom door ajar, showing off his body. It excited me until I could no longer control my desires. As soon as he disappeared behind the curtain, I stripped to nothing and followed him into the warm water. He pulled me in his arms, and time stopped. I lost myself in him.

After what seemed an eternity in each other's arms, I came back to my senses and remembered I was supposed to meet Andrea at five. I felt a little dizzy when I got up from the bed, but it soon passed. We quickly jumped into the shower once again, and by the time we were ready to leave, it was already five. He left for the bar, and I went to meet Andrea. I had some explaining to do.

When I reached the office, she was sitting and patiently waiting for me. It took us a half hour to take care of our business. With our plane tickets in our pockets and our bills paid up, we headed to our room.

We were told we would be leaving at nine o'clock in the morning by the same bus we had arrived in, which would take us directly to the airport in time for our flight. When we passed in front of the boutique, Andrea decided on a shopping spree. I left her there and went to the room to start packing.

Thirty minutes later, a big bag made its way in, followed by Andrea. "My god! Did you buy the whole boutique?" I asked her, laughing.

"There it is! Three hundred seven dollars' worth of gifts for everybody back home," she said proudly as she lifted the bag up to my eyes.

"I guess that's what happens when you have a big family and lots of friends," I went on while packing my suitcases. I wanted to pack quickly so that my night would be free.

"There's a single's party at the disco at seven. Devin told me they had drinks for everyone, and those coming without a date are given one," she said as she grabbed her suitcase to begin packing.

"Don't tell me you want to start another relationship with someone now!" I teased.

"Of course not, but don't you think it would be fun to see what it's all about? Plus, Devin is in charge of it all."

"I see. Well, its fine with me."

We talked a while, and then I hopped into the shower. When I was finished in the bathroom, Andre had finished packing. "Louise, when should our luggage be at the baggage depot?"

"They said one hour before leaving," I answered her while putting on my white silky dress.

"I guess one of us should ask for a wake-up call at the hostess desk tonight. Will you be coming in tonight?"

"Most likely, yes," I replied, but deep down inside, I was lying to myself. I wanted Yoann to lead me into temptation but deliver me from all evil. In other words, I was still a mess, trying so hard to hold myself together. Then I went on to say, "I'll drop a note at the hostess desk for the wake-up call." I was ready and eager to leave.

"Are you going somewhere now?" she asked, observing me.

"I want to go on the beach to watch the evening sunset. I'll meet you at seven at the disco, okay?" I looked at my watch: it was already six fifteen.

"I'll be there! See you later," Andrea replied as she went into the bathroom for her shower.

I walked along the seashore, admiring the horizon, where the sun was slowly setting. It gave such a beautiful look to the water, almost making it look as if diamonds were floating on the sparkling surface. I realized I had found the antidote injection for civilization I was searching for, but time was against me, leaving me only wonderful memories, which would eventually bring me back to Club Vacation— maybe not here, but at another location. I gazed out as the sun set behind the horizon, casting a colorful glow in the already dark sky.

I slowly made my way back, still enjoying the sight and the feel of the cool sand on my feet. Little lights strewn along the pathway, made it quite romantic to walk around the village at night. I reached the pool area and bumped into Alain. My heart raced at the sight of him. I didn't feel like having trouble of any sort. "Hello, Alain," I said nicely enough.

"Hello, Louise. Do you have a few minutes to spare? There's something I must say to you."

"Well, yes, I do have a few minutes," I told him, wondering what he had to tell me that was so important.

"I would like to apologize to you for the way I treated you the last few days. God knows you don't deserve that kind of treatment. You're such a sweet girl. Maybe everything is my fault. I don't know whether you will ever understand how much I wanted you, how much I loved you. Even now, it still bothers me. I spoke with Yoann again, and he told me you two were only good friends—and you were only sleeping at his place, just like you said. I guess I should have believed you when you told me, but my jealousy blinded me to anything you said. I'm sorry, but I thought you were the kind of girl who went with anyone. I guess I was wrong."

I was stunned by this turn of events between the two of us. I felt sorry for him, knowing it was not all true, but it was the only way to make him understand the way life was. And Yoann had understood that before both of us. Alain's jealousy turned everything into ugliness.

I decided to leave it at that and accept his apologies. "Alain, I'm happy to see I haven't lost your friendship. In your own way, you told me how much you loved me. I couldn't be angry with you about it, but now I am really happy to see you came to par with yourself."

He kissed me quickly on the cheek and then walked away before I could say another word.

I hurried to the disco. Andrea would surely be mad at me, and with good reason. It had been twice in a very short time that I had arrived late at our rendezvous. But she was understanding and forgave me right away. "If you want a cocktail," she told me, "you have to go see Devin. He's over there in the corner." She pointed to where Devin was standing. There must have been over 180 single people in the entire village, all gathered for the party and looking forward to having a good time.

I was standing near the dance floor, admiring some of the dancers' gracefully, when I felt someone breathing down my neck. I turned around, ready to strike, but it was only Gregory. "There you are, pretty face," he said, his glazed eyes gazing down my neckline. "I thought we were supposed to meet here last night. Where did you run to?" he said slurring his words.

I replied, "I was in here last night, my dear, but only for a short while. It was early when I called it a night."

"Come on, Louise. I saw you leave the main bar with that big guy, that Samson. When I came, neither of you were here."

"Gregory, don't tell me you've been following me."

"Oh, me? I'd never do a thing like that. You know me! It just happened by coincidence, that's all."

That pissed me off, and I had to say it. "Well, let me tell you something, fellow, before you begin to get ideas in this big head of yours. Time hasn't changed any of the feelings I never had for you, so don't think because you see me here, you're gonna work your way to my bed, because you're not. Got the message?"

He said, "I always knew you had quite a good sense of humor. Keep the good act, kid. Now, I have to meet this very exciting chick." He glanced at his watch. "I'll see you a little later. Oh, and by the way, if I don't get the chance to see you before you leave, have a nice trip back. Don't forget to give the message to Andrea." He left as fast as he came. I didn't think he would give up so easily, but I was glad he did. Guys were all the same: when they know nothing would be gained with one girl, they hopped to the next one. I wondered whether I was lucky or naive to think Yoann was an exception.

I didn't have time to finish my introspection. Andrea pushed her way through the dance floor, grabbing me hurriedly in the process. We were pushed very close to one another, which made it hard to dance but easy to chat. "What was all that talk with you and Gregory? You didn't seem very happy to see him." She had this little teasing smile in the corner of her mouth.

"Well, you know how men can be. He may have all the necessary attributes to charm a girl—the blue eyes, jet-black hair, baby face, and long legs to support so much muscle—but a woman in love is a woman in love. Plus, the guy gets on my nerves. All he sees is flesh, not an ounce of brains."

"Yeah, I know what you mean."

The party was going full blast. Everybody seemed to have a great time. The GSs arranged everything so that all the singles were able to get acquainted. It was a very nice way to get to meet people.

Dinner was right around the corner when Andrea asked me if I was hungry. I was starving. Devin had to be in the cleanup squad, so we decided to make our way to the dining room in order to keep places for our loved ones. As we were approached by the hostess to be seated, we were surprised to find out that Yoann had already reserved a table for the four of us. It was a complete dinner à la cart, which mean the full-course dinner served the French way, including two entrees and scrumptious desserts. Like always, we were delighted with the food and a little sad to leave it all behind. We finished our dinner over cognac at the main bar, the four of us cheering for friendship and love. Many of the GSs we met through our week stopped by to wish us a good trip back home. At that point, tears rolled down my cheeks as I thought about the many friends we had made in so short a time. I tried to dry them as fast as they came so Yoann didn't notice them. I had to be seen as a brave; it was very important to me.

Andrea and Devin decided to watch the show, but Yoann and I opted for a walk on the beach. It was our last night together, so we wanted to make the best of it. We walked along under the moonlight, hand in hand. I wish I never had to let him go and that time would one day bring us together forever, sheltered by his strong arms. I had tightness in the pit of my stomach that grew stronger as each day of the week had passed, and now it was at a peak. I knew it was causing my worries, which was really a smooth word to describe the fright I felt in my gut about leaving this place—and leaving Yoann. I was more than confused about my feelings, which had reached a turning point in the middle of the week. My life seemed to have changed from then on.

While walking along, I said. "Yoann, I have to tell you. I am so afraid of the future. I'm not sure of anything anymore. I don't even know how to handle this separation." I held his hand tighter as if doing so would give me more strength.

With passion in his words and in his touch, Yoann said, "Louise, darling, we will have to make the best of what we have and make sure what we found together grows even stronger as the days go by."

We walked silently for a while along the pathways leading to the beach. The moon was so bright in the sky, and the little lights along the paths made the garden look more beautiful than I had seen them before. Maybe it was because my eyes were taking it all in for the last time. Sometimes when something is taken for granted, the eyes do not see all the beauties that lie right in front of them. Tonight, it looked so good. As I gazed up at all this beauty, a question formed in my head and added to the tightness in my stomach. "Do you think you would be able to one day give up this kind of life the club provides for you?"

"Louise—I love calling that sweet name." He smiled and went on. "I believe everything can become possible, that is if one believe in it but the time for these thoughts has not come yet. Be patient, and all will fall into place. Three months from now, we will meet again, and that will be a good time to talk about those things." I thought of his words for a minute and believed it was the only choice I had for the time being. Time was the only thing that could answer my questions.

The only sounds on the beach were the waves splashing on the shore. The only light sources were the moon and the lightning bugs, something I had never seen before. The setting was perfect for our last night. It was a night to remember, as the love stories say. He talked to me about his beliefs in life, his fear, and his love. I sat next to him, content with his words, his presence, and the surroundings that seemed to hug us in its darkened embrace. I was happy, and the tightness in my gut gave way to great warmth coursing throughout my body. For a moment, I imagined I would feel this kind of sensation if I were in paradise. The wind brought us sounds of music from the opening of the Olympics ceremony back at the amphitheater. Time passed much too quickly—it was already a quarter to twelve.

"What time are you leaving in the morning?" Yoann asked me as he got up.

"Oh, gosh! That just reminded me! I need a wake-up call from the hostess desk for tomorrow at seven thirty."

"Don't worry. I'll wake you up in the morning. Just leave it to me," he assured me, taking my hand and pulling me to my feet. We walked hand in hand, reached his room, and made our way in. The little voice in my head told me not to this time, but my legs kept moving. I was not in control anymore.

As soon as the door was closed, he pulled me to him and kissed me passionately. I drank from him as if for the last time in my life, hungrily and with a passion I could not control. We slowly undressed one another, and then he took my hand and led me to the shower.

The water felt warm on my naked skin, and with his body so close to mine, I felt hot. He brought me to his bed, still glistening with water. My strong feelings forced me to speak out. "I love you so much, Yoann," I whispered in his ears. I wanted each second with him to last a lifetime. I lost myself in his sweetness and closed my eyes to the reality, drowning in the loving coziness of this unforgettable moment.

THIRTY-ONE

Standing on the edge of time

I was standing on the edge of a cliff, but really, there seemed to be something very strange happening. The cliff surrounded me, but fog kept me from seeing the edge of it, and there was this hand coming from nowhere that kept shaking me, pushing me off balance and almost throwing me off the edge of the cliff. I was trying to scream, but no sound came out of my mouth because my throat was so dry I couldn't utter a sound. I tried and tried to scream, but to no avail, and all this fright that enveloped me like a dark veil made my whole body tremble. The hand became more demanding and more aggressive, and just as I was about to fall off the cliff, my eyes opened and met Yoann's warm, securing presence. It was his hand shaking me out of my sleep.

"Wake up, darling. It's already seven thirty."

I couldn't believe it. My vacation was finished—it was time to leave. Then I thought of my luggage, which had to be at the baggage depot at eight. I quickly jumped out of bed.

I took a quick shower, and while Yoann took his, I got myself together. we were ready to leave at ten minutes to eight. Just as I was about to open the door to my room to get my luggage, Devin opened it. "Oh, there you are. I was about to come looking for you after dropping off Andrea's luggage."

I said, "You know how I go now. I'm always on time." Yoann smiled at him.

"Yeah, that's why I didn't make up my mind earlier to collect them," Devin said, smirking back at me. We let him out with Andrea's heavy suitcases. I went in with Yoann, finished packing, and handed him my suitcases.

While I was packing, Andrea sat down next to my suitcase. "I was beginning to wonder where you were for a minute. I thought I was going to take the plane alone!" she joked.

"How can you say a thing like that? You know I have to go back home. Plus, I wouldn't do that to you. You know that." I gave her a friendly punch on her chin. She responded by a friendly punch to my stomach. Upon seeing this, Yoann asked us if we needed a referee. We all burst out laughing.

While we were waiting for the boys to return from the baggage depot, I went into the bathroom to put on my traveling clothes. Andrea told me about the previous night's event. Surprising me, she said, "I was given a letter for you last night."

"Aren't you gonna tell me from whom?" I was dying of curiosity.

"From Alain. He gave it to me last night in the disco. He told me he looked all over for you and even came to the room to see if you were there. He seems crazy about you. What the hell did you do to him?"

"I wish I knew. You'd better believe I won't do it again. Or maybe it's not what I did but more what I didn't do. Thanks for taking it. It will give me something to read on the bus to the airport."

"I put it in your purse." At that moment, the boys came back from the depot.

We took a last look around the room to see whether anything had been forgotten, took out traveling bags and handbags, and then made our way to have our last breakfast together. It was already eight thirty when we entered the restaurant. I took a last look at all the goodies surrounding me and made a final feast while seated next to my loved one. I dreaded the moment when we would have to say goodbye. I wanted to be strong in front of Yoann. Maybe that was why I took so much time to eat my breakfast. I wanted the last half hour to last forever, but I couldn't fool the tingling moving up my leg. I could see by Andrea's expression, and she was equally as sad to leave Devin and this paradise.

With the tingling now moving up my other leg, I couldn't stop the tears that came to my eyes. One rolled down my cheek, and Yoann noticed it right away. He took his napkin and tenderly wiped it away in a gesture that seemed to want to take away all my sadness. Even he couldn't do that now.

"I guess it's time we get going," Andrea suggested, looking at me sadly.

"Yeah, I guess you're right." We reluctantly got up and walked two by two toward the entrance of the village.

The bus was already waiting for us, and that tingling in my legs did not wear off. I simply needed to sit with him again, but I knew the only seat I would be taking was on the bus. I saw our luggage at the bus's opened side compartment. Yoann walked up to the side of the bus while Andrea and Devin stayed a little farther behind. He took me in his arms and looked me in the eyes. "Louise, I want you to be strong in the months to come. Always remember that everything is possible, and I will be here waiting to meet you in three months. The people around you will try to put doubt in your mind, but don't let them. Keep your own confidence and strength. And remember that I care for you so much that I cannot use words to express it." He hugged me tightly, kissed me tenderly, and then looked at me again and whispered, "I'll be missing you, you know." His eyes looked watery.

"I'll miss you so much." The tingling I felt was gone. I guessed I really needed that last hug to make me feel better.

Our attention was taken away by someone shouting my name. "Louise, Andrea! Wait for me!" We all turned in the direction of the person coming at us and waving a bottle of 7 Up in the air. It was Cenny. When I saw him coming like that, as sad as I was at that moment, I couldn't stop a big smile from coming to my lips. When he had our attention, he took his own sweet time to reach us, that eternal smiling face turned toward me. "So you were going to leave without saying goodbye, huh?" He pointed his finger accusingly at Andrea and me.

"Oh, Cenny, you know how it goes sometimes. No grudges, I hope." I gave him my sweetest smile, hoping to be forgiven.

"Okay, okay, it's all right. I just want to give you this bottle. It can get very dry on a long trip sometimes. If you do get thirsty, you'll be properly equipped," he said handing me the bottle.

It was so sweet of him, and I didn't know what to say.

"Thank you Cenny. That's very nice of you." I placed the bottle to my chest and kissed him goodbye on both cheeks. Andrea did the same.

The bus blew its horn, announcing it was departure time. Right before we got on the bus, the chief of the village came by to wish us a good trip, and he said he hoped we had enjoyed our stay in the village. We thanked him warmly and hopped on the bus. Yoann stared at my window for our final goodbyes, and Devin did the same with Andrea. It was so hard to say farewell to the ones we loved, but I was stronger than I imagined I could be. Andrea couldn't stop crying; maybe that was why I didn't. Someone had to stay clearheaded, even though my stomach was a very hard knot. Yoann gave me a final kiss through the window side of the bus. The bus slowly began to move, with Andrea and I waving goodbye through the back window. It was a good thing Yoann didn't see me then. Tears streamed down my face, and I couldn't stop them. Andrea was no help—she was like a Madonna.

About twenty minutes later, Andrea had cried herself to sleep, and I seemed to have lost the ability to feel. I tried to focus all my attention on the beauty of the hills and mountains as the bus moved farther and farther from my loved one and his paradise.

At one point, I remembered Alain's letter sitting in my handbag. I reached for it, ripped open the enveloped, and read.

Dear Louise.

Confession from the heart is never easy, and it's not simple when love is involved. You know how much I love you and wanted you, but still you lied to me. I was at your room last night, and you were not there. At first I did believe you when you told me you and Yoann were only friends. What a fool I've been. Girls like you don't deserve to be loved. I know what Yoann has over me, and believe me, before I leave this village, he and I will have it out. At first I thought you were too good for me, but you fooled me so well. Even though I wish never to see you again, the hurt will remain. For what it's worth, I can only wish you well.

Alain

That was all I needed to feel dreadful. I decided to not let this letter affect me. I balled it up, threw it out the window, and then leaned back for comfort. I tried for a few hours of sleep before we reached the airport.

Andrea and I were awoken by the noise going on in the little city of Puerto Vallarta. A few more miles, and we would reach the airport. We talked a while and marveled at the scenery and the way the people lived here. The bus stopped at the entrance of the airport. A porter arrived who knew exactly where to lead us when I told him Aero Mexico. In no time we boarded the airplane, and in a last farewell to this magnificent country, I glanced at the horizon to drink in the beauty before setting foot on the plane that would take me back to my "building city," as I called it.

The flight home was very smooth. Andrea and I discussed our trip again and again, never bored to go into the little details. We exchanged deep thoughts about our loved ones. When we landed in New York, we were so tired after all the traveling and the routine at immigration and customs. We hopped in the car and headed for a restaurant for a quick dinner.

I dropped her home and hurried back to my house. I couldn't wait to put my head on my pillow and sleep in my own bed. Mom and Dad were in the living room, waiting up for me to hear all about my magnificent trip. When I finally reached my room that night to sleep, after giving a good rundown on my trip to my parents—excluding my intimate relationship—I finally let out a sigh of exhaustion as I relaxed my body under the covers. My mind was restless and kept going back to the club and Yoann. I wondered what he was doing at that minute.

I supposed I would think those thoughts often enough in the next few months.

Yoann once said, "Be true to yourself," so here is my confession. The truth is Andrea and I was never true blondes. Thank God for women's hair coloring.

I kept seeing the beauty of the surroundings, the wonderful GSs so eager to please and full of happiness, and the activities that were so fascinating for me. I fell asleep dreaming I was still in Playa, Mexico, surrounded by flowers, the sound of the ocean, and Yoann.

Days turned into weeks. One month had already passed since my trip to Mexico. I didn't return to the Quick Rap Restaurant, not even to explain my situation to Larry. I started working at my father's new clothing business, avoiding my boyfriend at all cost. To my surprise, I enjoyed the work. I'd met with Andrea twice since we'd returned, both of us too busy and wrapped up in our own lives to take off more time. Yoann and I regularly wrote to each other. He even called me twice since my return. He missed me as much as I missed him. His plans definitely included him coming to New York after the end of his season. The thought of his coming made me so eager. At one point, I had to fight those thoughts away from my mind in order to go on with my everyday routine. I did feel strong in my heart, but sometimes I wiped a tear or two and tried to keep busy so that the tingling in my legs didn't come back. I kept these thoughts away from my loved one.

One morning, I woke up and decided to try my luck. I took the day off, got myself ready, and headed down to the Club Vacation office. I filled out an application form to be a GS, waited a while, and had an interview with one of the personnel employees. We chatted for at least half an hour. She was a very animated person who was warm and funny. Everyone in the club seemed to be so dynamic and communicative. I left her office ready to conquer the world, even though she stressed on the fact that the waiting list to become a GS was long. I didn't know what would become of it, but at least I was giving it a try.

I was still avoiding seeing my boyfriend at home. The truth was I didn't know what to say or how to say it to him.

THIRTY-TWO

Yes, he arrived in New Your, New Your

Time went by slowly, and finally Yoann was making his way to me. We had so much to talk about, as well as decisions and plans to make. Having him near me was the most exquisite sensation. I felt so light and happy. I had no worries in the world besides a ringing phone, but that eventually stopped. I assumed my now ex-boyfriend got the message given that he was living in another state. I was happy to hear Yoann was on his way to New York.

Finally, the big day: Yoann was here in New York with me! We visited the whole city, saw plays and movies, and ate at wonderful restaurants. My father was a tremendous boss. He gave me more than enough time off to enjoy myself with the man I loved. Now there was no doubt about it: Yoann was the one and only. It had been a shock at first to my parents to meet Yoann and hear about the fact that we were both in love with one another, but time had a way of smoothing matters, and he was so charming with them. They fell for him too.

Yoann's life in the club was guaranteed. I loved him so much, but the only guarantee I could give was to myself: to never take another call from that former boyfriend of mine.

I could not afford Yoann coming to me and getting into a brawl with my ex in the middle of New York City. I had to assure him there was no other.

Yoann said something to me I would never forget. "The worst kind of business is unfinished business." I was more than happy to indicate this notion to my boyfriend by never again taking his calls. Was that selfish or just human? Either way, I was going to find out.

Yoann was already on his third week of vacation. One morning, the phone rang for me. It was Club Vacation calling to ask if I would be ready to leave for a village in a week or so. I couldn't believe my ears. I had made it! They had chosen me! In my haste, I almost forget to ask whether Tahiti was possible for my first village, but at the last minute, I got hold of myself to remember the crucial question. The girl told me she would have to get back to me on that matter. I crossed my fingers. Yoann was leaving shortly for Tahiti as his next village. Wouldn't it be something if I would be able to go too? When I hung up, I couldn't hold it in. I started dancing and singing my happiness, grabbed Yoann by the neck, and told him about the good news. At that information, he joined me in dancing and singing like two little children. We finally ended up in each other's arms, hugging and laughing with joy.

A week and a half later, with both our suitcases comfortably seated in the back trunk of my father's car, my dream had finally come true. I was with Yoann, scheduled to leave for the most exotic and beautiful village Club Vacation controlled: Tahiti.

I always thought nice endings belonged in stories, but for once, the fairy tale was becoming a reality. Hand in hand, with laughter and happiness playing in our shining eyes, we settled in the back seat of the car, on our way to the fantastic future reserved for us. "Are you ready, my dearest?" he asked, smiling.

"I will always be ready if you are by my side, love!" I gave my warmest smile to the one I had chosen to be my man for the rest of my life.

Strangely, while smiling to myself, I never had to think or call Yoann Black Beauty ever again—because Black Beauty was all mine. For as long as time allows, I was going to follow this road to be with the man I loved. I knew the road of grace was not paved with gold and diamonds, but with triumph and mercy.

As spring, summer, fall, and winter passed, we stayed working together in many of the other Club Vacation villages around the world.

Mr. Yoann Pesant is best known for his Bahamian music. His sophisticated Bahamian films are excellent at preserving the Arawak and Caribs dynasties that once flourished not only the Bahamas' seven hundred islands but throughout the entirety of the Caribbean. His work depicts in depth a long-forgotten culture of the Bahamian people. Mr. Pesant resides between Nassau, New Providence, and Quebec, Canada.

To know more about Mr. Yoann Pesant, visit his websites:
http://gouddaa.50webs.com/News.html
Facebook: Gouddaa Bahamas
YouTube:
    https://www.youtube.com/watch?v=yM9I39XuYxk
    http://www.youtube.com/watch?v=iMwTi8IEjhs
    https://www.youtube.com/watch?v=aUrhmLY0L1Q
    https://www.youtube.com/watch?v=Y3sy5zpR_wU